Social work 2000

John Muir

SOCIAL WORK 2000
The future of social work in a changing society

Ronald G. Walton

Longman
London and New York

LONGMAN GROUP LIMITED

Longman House
Burnt Mill, Harlow, Essex, CM20 2JE, ENGLAND AND ASSOCIATED
COMPANIES THROUGHOUT THE WORLD

*Published in the United States of America
by Longman Inc., New York*

© Longman Group Limited 1982

All rights reserved. No part of this publication may be
reproduced, stored in a retrieval system, or transmitted
in any form or by any means, electronic, mechanical,
photocopying, recording, or otherwise, without the
prior permission of the Copyright owner.

First published 1982

BRITISH LIBRARY CATALOGUING IN PUBLICATION DATA

Walton, Ronald G.
  Social work 2000.
  1. Social service—Great Britain
  I. Title
  361.3'0941   HV245

ISBN 0-582-29622-6

LIBRARY OF CONGRESS CATALOGING IN PUBLICATION DATA

Walton, Ronald Gordon.
  Social work 2000.

  Bibliography: p.
  Includes index.
  1. Social service–Great Britain. 2. Social prediction. I. Title. II. Title: Social work two thousand.
HV245.W26   361.3'0941   82-12
ISBN 0-582-29622-6   AACR2

Printed in Great Britain by
William Cloves (Beccles) Ltd
Beccles and London

CONTENTS

Preface and acknowledgements vi
List of abbreviations ix
Introduction 1

1. A world perspective 4
2. The United Kingdom – economic developments and the Welfare State 9
3. Personal social services 16
4. Social work and the Welfare State 33
5. Social work methods and practice 45
6. Manpower, structures and training 62
7. Concluding discussion 84
   Appendices 94
   A Trends in selected social services in England and Wales 94
   B Social services department staff in England and Wales 96
   C Numbers of students entering training and qualifying 98
   D Great Britain population projections – mid-1979 base 99

References and Bibliography 101
Index 107

PREFACE AND ACKNOWLEDGEMENTS

This book is intended as a contribution to the continuing debates about social work in our society. In late 1980 a Social Work Inquiry was established by the DHSS under the chairmanship of Peter Barclay and based at the National Institute for Social Work. The inquiry reflects a fairly widespread concern inside and outside social work. The rough plan and general comment of the book was developed 1979–80 and the opportunity to write it was provided by a period of study leave granted by University College, Cardiff. A draft was completed in November 1980 before the Social Work Inquiry had started working and at a time when further cuts in public expenditure had just been announced. At a time of great pressure on the staff of personal social services and of cuts to services affecting some of the worst-off members of society it is still important to focus on medium- and long-term objectives and issues despite a necessary preoccupation with coping with present problems.

As well as being indebted to University College, Cardiff for the time to undertake background research and writing, I owe thanks to colleagues in the Department of Social Administration and School of Social Work, for their stimulation and influence over recent years and for sharing my workload during my absence. The debt owed to present and former colleagues is always substantial, and the influence although less tangible is just as forceful as that from acknowledged publications and research – such influence includes that of residential, field and training staff in personal social services whose experience and views about their work and the social services prevent social work teachers from losing a grip on the reality of day-to-day caring and providing services. David Fowler, of the School of Social Work, read the manuscript and I am indebted to him for a number of valuable comments. Staff of the DHSS and

Preface and acknowledgements

Welsh Office were extremely helpful in providing the most recent statistics for personal social services.

As a member of a social work teaching group, I should acknowledge the possibility that my views are biased by an identification with social work interests. However, I have tried, through the arguments presented, to avoid assuming that social work is in some absolute form good and must therefore be expanded. But no apologies are made for starting from an assumption that on the whole social workers are useful members of society and that without them, in present circumstances, there would be a good deal more misery in the community. Equally, I start from an assumption that generally State intervention in the lives of citizens should be kept within bounds and be with their consent and have good justifications where it does occur. It is not simply a question of more or less social work, but what kinds of social work and how related to broad welfare institutions and society.

In presentation, every effort has been made to keep the text uncluttered and to present clear information and lines of argument. The main sources of material are shown in the list of references and bibliography. In many cases, the books referred to are indicative of the kind of material available, rather than a complete or exhaustive list. As far as possible, technical jargon has been avoided, and the text should be as comprehensible to the general reader as to social work and social service specialists. I apologise in advance to those whose work is relevant but is not considered or examined in detail. Among these are economists advocating voucher schemes in welfare and Marxists who see the 'welfare crisis' as a crisis of the capitalist state. Both these groups draw attention to the problems of the Welfare State in analyses broadly similar to the one presented here. In their prescriptions, the voucher/choice in welfare group would probably put greater pressure on personal social services and social workers; the more universalist tendencies of Marxists would most likely reduce the need for social workers. However, in whichever directions welfare policies move in the next few years – they are unlikely to move to the extreme ends of the policy spectrum – the broad analysis outlined here would still hold good. Detailed consideration of the Probation Service is omitted. Not because it is considered unimportant, or not a part of social work, but because the main lines of argument in relation to social services departments apply equally to probation. Any large-scale shift away from custodial care will have major implications for probation services. As in

Preface and acknowledgements

local authorities, there will be an extended range of service and differentiation in the use of manpower. Also changes in the scale and administration of broad Welfare State services will have similar implications for the probation services. Unless it, too, adapts and changes, it runs the danger of becoming an anachronistic and inefficient relief and support organisation. Fortunately, there are signs that despite the present flirtation with the Law and Order philosophy to protect the present level of resources, innovatory practice thinking and reform objectives are still flourishing albeit in a rather subdued fashion.

In the preparation of the manuscript, my thanks are due to my wife for writing out the text legibly for typing, and to Mrs Sheila Spencer for undertaking the typing of the first draft and final manuscript, completed in the summer and autumn of 1981.

Ron Walton
October, 1981

LIST OF ABBREVIATIONS

BASW	British Association of Social Workers
CAB	Citizens Advice Bureau
CCETSW	Central Council for Education and Training in Social Work
CQSW	Certificate of Qualification in Social Work
CRSW	Certificate in Residential Social Work
CSS	Certificate in Social Service
DHSS	Department of Health and Social Security
IEA	Institute of Economic Affairs
NISW	National Institute of Social Work
OECD	Organisation for Economic Co-operation and Development
PQS	Post-Qualifying Studies
PSSC	Personal Social Services Council

For my parents
and
my three daughters

INTRODUCTION

That social work is in a state of crisis is taken to be axiomatic by many within and outside social work. A crisis statement usually contains much vagueness and precious little enlightenment. Western civilisation and capitalism are also supposed to be in a stage of crisis. Jeremiahs and Cassandras will always find reasons for assuming that the end of the world is at hand and the possibility of a nuclear holocaust feeds into social hysteria and depression, with subsequent panic or paralysis. Every age has its problems, but nothing is to be gained by elevating them into a crisis category which prevents men from thinking and acting with intelligence and responsibility.

Change in its infinite forms and degrees, not crisis, is a concept which encourages both present modes of thought and action but also extends our minds beyond immediate horizons, and enables us individually and collectively to plan to overcome present problems and search out reformulated goals and means of achieving them. Social work has been said to be at the crossroads and its very survival has been called into question. The context for the present attempt to map out future prospects is the awareness that significant shifts in culture, social institutions and technologies are in train which provide both new problems and new opportunities in the development of social work. To ignore these changes is to risk consigning social work to a moribund state, maladapted to society in the immediate future and unresponsive to challenges which lie ahead in the next two decades.[1]

This project, then, is an attempt to explore the directions of social change over the next twenty years and their indications for positive changes in social work as a relatively minor but significant social institution. The period of a quarter century has been chosen because it sets the horizon further ahead than the normal social service planning periods of central and local government and yet is not

Introduction

so far into the future as to lose touch with reality. Governments and business corporation are already using twenty to thirty years ahead as longer-term boundaries in considering energy use and technological possibilities. Since investment in capital social service resources has a gestation period of up to a decade and may then remain relatively fixed for periods of 20–100 years, a tentative planning horizon of twenty years is not a long period. Given that use of more flexible human resources is determined substantially by the structure of capital resources, the arguments for a twenty-year horizon grow even stronger.

A misconception could arise that in projecting forwards twenty years, the enterprise is either too mechanistic or a variant of crystal ball gazing. This would be a mistake. In using such evidence as is available to describe possible changes, the aim is not to produce a blueprint for social work at X point in the future. It is, rather, to describe some of the major parameters, with their possibilities and constraints, of which social work will need to take account.[2] Possibly in doing so some major shifts in direction will emerge. If it is possible to define, even fairly broadly, some of those directions, then medium-term planning with a continuous rolling period of 3–5 years, becomes both more informed and more flexible. The worst position is where large stocks of capital become locked into patterns of service which are likely to become quickly outmoded.

The major changes which will be surveyed are: population; technology and economic development; social welfare (social security, housing, education, health); personal social services; political institutions. Implications for social work can then be analysed, taking into account the present use of resources and the effects of changes already taking place. Implications from the longer-term analysis for medium-term analysis and planning can then be formulated. Although, in a necessarily brief form, the project has to start with world-wide developments to provide a background scenario to developments in the OECD and then in Great Britain, whenever possible hard data will be used, but it is in the nature of the enterprise that alternative assumptions will have to be made at various points. By this means it is possible to escape the limitations of analysis based only on population projections[3] without being seduced by a naïve utopianism. Social workers should be able to play a more intelligent and effective part in negotiating the boundaries and constitution of social work to society. As in the past no small part of this will be in influencing and being influenced by the values and perceptions of other groups and social institutions. This

Introduction

social reflexiveness or lack of it will determine whether social work joins the ranks of aged and atrophied institutions or emerges reshaped with a renewed vigour.

NOTES

1. The initial stimulus to take a longer term view came from a series of articles in the *Financial Times*: Planning in an age of uncertainty, *Financial Times*, 1979.
2. *Interfutures*, OECD, Paris, 1979. The OECD report contrasts the term 'prospective analysis' with 'forecasting' in the traditional sense, p. 3.
3. A balanced use of population projection is to be found in *Population and The Social Services*, Report by the Central Policy Review Staff, HMSO, 1977.

Chapter One
A WORLD PERSPECTIVE

The tasks facing the next twenty to twenty-five years are critical for both developed and developing nations. Increases in population and economic development in the South will engender strains on the economies of the North as they accommodate themselves to new patterns of development aid and international trade. The pressures on energy resources, food and raw materials will occur in a context where there are no new continents to be developed, focusing our attention on the need for critical technological innovation as the major way of overcoming world problems in conjunction with efforts to develop social institutions which will adapt to and manage the impact of social, economic and technical change. Whilst the will and ability to overcome the problems of the next twenty years will not depend upon a minor social institution such as social work, whether or not social work as part of the welfare system can make a worthwhile contribution to society depends upon its awareness of structural changes in the world and national economies. Economics and politics used to be part of the normal curriculum for social work courses until the 1950s. Now they are notable for their absence, except where studied under the umbrella of social policy. Reinstating the importance of economic and political issues in social work training would be a part of the agenda arising from this project.

Critical world issues identified by OECD (1979:410) for the next twenty years are:
1. The energy transition.
2. The search by developed countries for national policies adapted to the new context.
3. Common efforts for the development of the Third World.
4. New forms of international cooperation.

A world perspective

As has the more recent Brandt Report, North–South (Independent Commission on International Issues 1980), and as the earlier *Limits to Growth*, Club of Rome reports (D. Meadows et al. 1972), the OECD report *Interfutures* (OECD 1979) identified the need for a balanced inter-relationship of development in the North and South. *Interfutures* and also Rostow in his *Getting From Here to There* (Rostow 1979) are considerably more optimistic about the capacity of world resources to sustain increasing populations, as long as the socio-political and technological problems can be surmounted, although Rostow argues that until an energy breakthrough occurs, the period up to the end of the century will retain the characteristics of a Fifth Kondratieff Upswing – prices of food and raw materials oscillating in a high range. Kondratieff's theory argues that periods of low prices after the opening up of major world food and raw material resources are followed by periods of rising prices as pressure on those resources builds up. In the post-war period the 1950s experienced relatively low prices followed by gradual pressure on food resources and raw materials in the 1960s. This *down swing* yielded to a firm *upswing* in the early 1970s with world-wide food shortages and the 1973 oil crisis. When may the next *downswing* be expected? Possibly when new cheap energy becomes available. But unlike earlier periods there are no vast unexplored regions or resources to exploit. Thus, the *downswing* is likely to be more dependent upon major technological breakthroughs than the previous *downswings*. The present *upswing* is likely to be characterised by periodic crises as world population grows from just under four billion in 1975 to approximately six billion in 2000, until major new technological innovation occurs in energy production.

At various points *Interfutures* identifies the changes which are highly likely to occur in the next twenty years in the developed countries as a part of the world climate as:

(a) A tendency to moderate economic growth rates.
(b) A restructuring of the economy; relative decline of staple industries (ship-building, cars, steel) and growth of new industry (micro-electronics – energy – communications) and the tertiary service sector.
(c) Pressures on the Welfare State as demands remain high but limited growth limits the capacity to meet demand.
(d) Emergence of new values, e.g. for increased participation and towards new types of community living.
(e) Greater demands on political institutions in responding to com-

plex problems, establishing policies and implementing them. Inflation and problems of distribution of the social product are key problems.

Any strategy for coping with the problems in a positive way, incorporating a long-term as well as a short-term politically pragmatic view, must combine a number of elements if it is to stand any chance of success. These elements would include (OECD 1979):
(a) The restoration of economic growth.
(b) The acceptance of structural change.
(c) Rejection of policies which exclude certain groups (e.g. racial minorities, young people, women, the handicapped) from the benefits of growth.
(d) Responsiveness to the demands and views of those groups likely to shape the future.
(e) Increased cooperation between the developed countries and between them and the less developed countries.

Of particular concern to social work in Great Britain is the evolution of the Welfare State in developed countries. In most developed countries public expenditure has reached near maximum acceptable limits. In the future, the total sum of public expenditure and within that total the proportion and type of welfare expenditure will be problematic and likely to be static or tending to small increases or decreases. Since expenditure on law and order, defence and health and social security are likely to be maintained and to give little room for manoeuvre, education, personal social service expenditure and housing seem most at risk of actual decline.

Yet the field of personal social services, encompassing social work, will be subject to increased demands because of a number of factors: increasing proportion of elderly people; effects of structural unemployment; protection of groups not likely to benefit from economic and social change; shifts in housing and social security policies; emergence of new values and conflicts of value which cause personal and family distress and may be seen as posing a threat to traditional shares values or growth-oriented economic values; new patterns of public/private provision where former sharp distinctions and boundaries are blurred; a much greater emphasis on efficiency and productivity; greater public participation in the development and management of services.

All these pressures are challenges which the public welfare system cannot afford not to confront creatively. Awareness of these likely trends leads to certain assumptions which underpin the analysis of the position in the UK. Firstly, economic growth is as vital to the interests of those dependent in some way on the Welfare State, as it is to the poor in less developed countries. In some social work circles economic growth is a dirty concept, but without such growth the weakest members of society are most likely to suffer in self-destructive battles over distribution of wealth and income. Secondly, social workers should not ally themselves to a latter-day Luddism. Structural change is vital to industry, and social workers will do far more to help those in need by supporting regional and sector policies which capitalise on new technologies and the service sector than fighting a rearguard action in defence of longstanding staple industries; social workers could have an important subsidiary role in alleviating short-term stress as a result of industrial change and in contributing to the consideration of the social impact of industrial change. Thirdly, social work can have a vital part to play in developing new forms of service involving joint provision with other Welfare State sectors (housing, health, social security), and with non-public services. Fourthly, many forms of services have remained relatively unchanged during the last thirty years. New patterns have managed to establish only a precarious hold as a proportion of all welfare resources. New forms of management and coordination must be developed which will foster a much speedier spread of more effective but newer types of service. Fifthly, social work has a much greater social development and planning role to play than hitherto. Traditionally social development has been considered as appropriate for less developed countries, but less so in developed countries (social planners and community workers have tended to have a tenuous grasp of social development planning). Economic and social development institutions and personnel must develop closer links in the future.

Objections may be put that these assumptions reflect a social democratic/conservative political ideology. Nothing could be further from the truth. The likely changes and developments in the next twenty years will throw up problems and issues which will face governments of whatever political colour. Where the analysis differs significantly from Marxist thinking is in viewing a declining role of profit in the developed countries as reflecting the pressures on global resources and increasing costs in exploiting them. This is not a peculiarly western capitalist problem but one shared by Eastern-bloc developed countries. Equally in all parts of the world, but particularly so in the developed countries as a vital part of meeting approaching problems and resolving them, governments should stimulate awareness of the issues if they are to activate public participation and agreement to possible solutions. Failure to promote informed public debate will inevitably produce defensive postures from social groups threatened by economic and social change. Political parties have notoriously ignored international issues in elections. In the future the inevitable interdependence of national and international issues must be presented to the electorate in democratic countries as a counterbalance to the usual insularity and short-sightedness of domestic politics.

The conflicts and tensions in western developed countries have been aggravated by the world recession 1980/81 with prospects of sluggish revival. Reactions so far have been political shifts to the right as in the USA and United Kingdom, troubled conditions in Sweden, the Netherlands and Italy, and a sharp turn to the left in France. The uncertainties of economic and political life, the emergence of newly aligned coalitions and, in the United Kingdom, the formation of the new Social Democratic Party in 1981, illustrate the search for more effective solutions and policies which will appeal to an increasingly diverse electorate. At present politicians have been caught unprepared for the speed of economic and technical changes which have led to a dramatic increase in unemployment since 1979. But there are already signs that political parties are educating themselves about patterns of economic and social change and becoming aware of more considered long-term responses as opposed to the adoption of panic measures. It is all the more important that in the United Kingdom where – to judge by governmental reaction to the inner-city riots of 1981 – political adaptation is least evident, social workers and other welfare workers, regularly in touch with the disadvantaged and those most at risk of economic and social marginality, should contribute effectively to the debate on how to achieve change without extensive damage to these individuals and groups. The social work contribution must not take a narrowly nationalistic form but take an international perspective. Midgley (1981) has shown how inappropriately social work has adapted to Third World conditions and how a more positive approach might be developed. The United Kingdom social worker has to adopt a three-way perspective: helping to achieve internal social change; doing this in a way which takes into account the economic and social needs of less developed countries; and promoting forms of social work and social services in Third World countries which we adapted to their economic, social and cultural needs.

Chapter two
THE UNITED KINGDOM – ECONOMIC DEVELOPMENTS AND THE WELFARE STATE[1]

ECONOMIC DEVELOPMENT

The United Kingdom as part of the OECD shares the problems and prospects of the developed world. Its situation is in some measure more difficult than that of many of its European partners and Japan. The sluggish response to structural adaptation, relatively low investment, high inflation, and an awkward competitive situation because of its oil resources and an over-valued currency, all point to a more difficult period of development, rather slower than many other developed countries. (See Table 1.)

It is important to note that the very moderate growth rates can be consistent with either structural change and the emergence of new consensus values, or lesser structural change and internal conflicts, dissatisfaction and persistent unemployment. The danger is that this latter pattern could evolve into a very slow growth neo-protectionist scenario. Present domestic economic policies are hav-

Table 1. Growth rates for a sample of OECD countries

	1975–90	1990–2000	1975–2000
USA	2.6	2.2	2.4
Germany	3.0	2.1	2.6
France	3.8	3.3	3.6
Italy	4.7	3.9	4.4
Japan	6.4	5.3	6.0
Netherlands	4.0	2.5	3.4
United Kingdom	2.8	2.6	2.7

Source: OECD *Interfutures*, Table 25, p. 131. (Omitting Australia, Belgium, Canada, Sweden, New Zealand.)

ing a severe impact on the level of economic activity, giving a lower base for future growth. Yet arguments about the serious social effects should not obscure the fact that most of the directions of change are vitally necessary in the medium and longer term. Any government of whatever party would hold to the same direction, but with variations in the emphasis given to demand management and alleviation of social consequences of economic change. The irony of the UK situation is that although the direction of economic change is right, some of the means of achieving it (e.g. a dogmatic monetarist policy) are producing the short-term changes of increasing inequalities and the growth of groups of social outcasts, which would normally be associated with giving absolute priority to economic growth. Medium- to long-term government strategies have so far failed to formulate social and economic policies in conjunction with each other. Unless there are more consistent and integrated policies developed, the likelihood is a series of bitter conflicts over distribution of incomes, particularly social incomes.

What then are the major changes which may be expected in the next twenty years or so?

1. *Economic growth*: fairly low rates of growth during the next two decades, possibly with a more sustained growth towards the end of the century.
2. *Structural change*: a relative decline in staple industry (steel, ship-building, textiles), expansion in energy (coal, nuclear power, solar, wind and ocean power), new industry (microelectronics, bio-technology, communications), the tertiary (service) sector and conservation.
3. *Employment*: relatively high rates of unemployment during the next decade (affecting particularly the young, women, coloured workers and older workers in regions of older industry), declining rather more in the final decade of the century.
4. *Regional imbalance*: Structural change is already affecting regions outside the South-East disproportionately. This is likely to continue during the next decade, and will only be partly modified by government policy.

The implications for government policy-making are clear in broad terms though frighteningly difficult to implement politically. Among the required policies are: new institutions to negotiate a broad consensus on incomes and prices; regional and sector planning; incentives to promote structural change; temporary (i.e. over the next decade) measures to make structural adaptation socially tolerable (income maintenance, training opportunities, strengthening the infrastructure of communications and public services); international cooperation to facilitate new international trading patterns North/South, rather than sliding into neo-protectionism.

These policies are critical for the development of the Welfare State, including personal social services and social work. Without moderate success in implementing them, services will be ground between the millstones of increased demands as a result of structural change and unemployment, and of fewer resources to meet the demands. Such pressures are already making themselves felt, and public services, including personal social services, cannot disown the responsibility of seeking economic policies which are balanced with social needs and development.

The Welfare State

In the OECD from the mid-1950s to the mid-1970s, public expenditure rose from an average of 28 per cent of GDP to 41 per cent of GDP. Figures for 1962 and 1975 are as set out in Table 2.

On average welfare expenditure is the largest element in public expenditure, constituting about 46 per cent of total public expenditure in OECD countries in 1975 compared with 37 per cent in 1950. In the United Kingdom, government expenditure was just under 50 per cent of GDP in 1975 and approximately 44 per cent in 1977–78. The Californian tax revolt of 1978–79 was echoed in the United Kingdom with the election of the Conservative government in May 1979. Reduction of public expenditure and taxes was a central part of the Conservative campaign, tied to a monetarist approach to control inflation. *The Government Expenditure Plans 1980–81 to 1983–84* (Cmnd. 7841 1980) differ slightly from the OECD calculations, but show essentially the same story as 1975–80 (see Tables 3 and 4).

Table 2. Public expenditure as a percentage of GDP at current prices

	1962	1975
United Kingdom	34.2	44.4
Sweden	32.7	49.4
Germany	33.6	42.1
France	36.3	40.3
United States	29.5	34.0

Source: OECD *Interfutures*, p. 176.

Table 3. United Kingdom ratio of public expenditure to GDP at market prices (%)

	Total public expenditure (including Debt interest)	Central Government expenditure in goods and services
1973–74	41.5	24.5
1974–75	46.5	26.0
1975–76	46.5	27.0
1976–77	45.0	25.5
1977–78	41.0	23.5
1978–79	42.5	23.0
1979–80	42.0	23.0

Source: Cmnd. 7841, p. 10.

Social services expenditure (social security, education, health and personal social services and housing) accounted for 56 per cent of public expenditure in 1976–77 and 58 per cent in 1977–78. Social security accounted for 27 per cent of Social services expenditure in 1976–77 and 26 per cent in 1977–78. Personal social services accounted for approximately one-seventh of health and personal social services expenditure in 1977–78 (£1.1 billion). Commitments to defence, law and order, employment services, the pressure on social security programmes (because of unemployment and the cost of pensions), and commitments to health services, taken together give the present government little room for manoeuvre in reducing public expenditure. Salaries and wages from the largest part of current expenditure when transfer payments are excluded, and the level of comparability awards are putting pressures on goods and service expenditure and also on capital formation. Within the social services sector given this public expenditure context, the most likely direction for attempts to reduce expenditure are in education, personal social services, and housing, combined with pressure to reduce indexing for social security benefits. It is clear that apart from social security the majority of this expenditure is by local authorities whose community-based services may suffer disproportionately. Total local authority expenditure fell from £20,678 million in 1974–75 to £18,365 million in 1978–79 (1979 prices), while central government expenditure, after reductions in 1976–78, rose sharply in 1978–79. Without economic policies which promote growth coupled with changes in priorities, the following results may be expected in the immediate years ahead:

Table 4. Social services expenditure by programme (at 1979 survey prices)

	1974–75		1978–79		1979–80		1980–81		Plans 1981–82		1982–83		1983–84	
	(£ m.)	(%)	(£ m.)	(%)	(£ m.)	(%)	(£ m.)	(%)	(£ m.)	(%)	(£ m.)	(%)	(£ m.)	(%)
Education	9,584	13	9,516	13	9,654	13	9,225	12	9,010	12	8,850	12	8,670	12
Housing	7,154	10	5,256	7	5,372	7	4,700	6	3,840	5	3,250	5	2,790	4
Health and personal social services	8,325	12	9,023	13	9,067	12	9,186	12	9,230	13	9,410	13	9,500	13
Social security	14,172	20	18,266	26	18,980	25	19,354	26	19,800	27	19,500	27	19,600	27
Total social services	39,238	55	42,061	59	42,983	57	42,465	57	41,880	57	41,010	57	40,560	57
Total public expenditure	71,575		72,106		75,100		74,551		73,300		71,700		71,400	

Source: Cmnd. 7841, p. 16.

Social work 2000

1. Deterioration of services in both quantity and quality at a time of increasing demand.
2. Reinforcement of traditional patterns of service rather than innovation.
3. Deterioration in the economic and social structure of the unemployed, low income families, single-parent families, the elderly, the mentally ill and the mentally and physically handicapped, racial minorities, i.e. the further growth of social outcast groups predicted by *Interfutures*.
4. Increasing homelessness.
5. Intentional reduction in research and monitoring activity to obscure these developments.
6. Increasing conflicts between: (a) the working population/the non-working population; (b) disadvantaged groups for a static or declining social income; (c) staffs of social services/service populations.
7. Increasing conflict over priorities over the whole range of public expenditure.
8. More rapid development of private social welfare as public services deteriorate.

The social effects of low growth or decline in the gross national product generate a response which is relatively uncoordinated and random in its effect, striking most severely at the weakest groups in society unable to use political power defensively. For the staffs of the broad social services, whichever government is in power, the medium- and long-term aim must be to support policies which lead to economic growth, among which must be included some form of income/prices policy however described and institutionalised. Campaigns to 'Fight the Cuts' may have a short-term role to play, but unless they are allied to constructive medium- to long-term economic policies, are likely to be viewed by politicians and the public as defensive moves aimed at protecting jobs and salaries rather than services.

Present short-term policies attain the worst outcome – slow or nil growth, and faltering structural change, achieved with a mix of policies that have all the damaging side-effects which might usually be associated with an over-riding priority of maximising economic growth. In contrast, the OECD *Interfutures* report argued for assumptions which anticipated a slowly increasing share of GNP for public consumption, at the same time as conflicts over the form and functions of the Welfare State in advanced industrial countries. One crucial part of this debate surrounds the role of the State as the

The United Kingdom—economic developments and the Welfare State

provider and regulator of services, as opposed to the role of the market in providing services. Several directions are possible: greater provision of welfare through occupational channels; greater provision through voluntary, non-profit-making organisations; greater provision by private profit-making organisations. None of these is mutually exclusive, and given the constraints on total public expenditure in the foreseeable future all should be explored to assess their potential contribution without leading to either a poor-quality public welfare system or unregulated poor-quality private services.

NOTE

1. Only a broad outline of welfare expenditure can be presented here. For a systematic treatment of the economics of the welfare state see I. Gough, *The Political Economy of the Welfare State*, Macmillan 1979.

Chapter three
PERSONAL SOCIAL SERVICES

DEMAND ON SERVICES

Potential demand for personal social services is extremely difficult to gauge with accuracy. Recent trends based on the numbers of people using services are not necessarily a good guide to the future. The way in which present resources relate to estimated need, i.e. the baseline for future developments, is an important constraining factor because of inelasticities in radically changing the quantity and the type of physical resources and also of the skills and working practices of human resources. Local authorities have traditionally relied on incremental approaches to the development of services, so that the organisational climate tends to perpetuate existing patterns of service. Yet some attempt at estimating future demand has to be undertaken, if only to avoid expensive investment which may be wasteful in a situation of declining demand. More positively, evidence of strong future demand yields the possibility of anticipating investment of resources, and, where possible, phasing out obsolescent service provision and incorporating innovatory service patterns.

There are three main factors in the generation of demand for personal social services: population size and composition; incidence of social problems; social policies in other parts of the Welfare State. Each of these factors involves complex study, and in this context it is only possible to offer some indicative comments, not a comprehensive analysis.

Population
Population is the most concrete and definite of the factors but it should be noted that future birth-rates are difficult to anticipate, themselves being related to economic and social trends and values.

Personal social services

Also, aggregate population figures for Great Britain do not indicate regional and sub-regional shifts in the distribution of population which are essential for planning services at the local level. The present discussion is based on the Report, *Population and the Social Services, 1977*, and all the figures relate to the 'central' projections detailed there. Appendix D gives mid-1979-based projections for Great Britain. These do not show major differences from Table 5; the broad trends are very similar.

It is in the 0–15 age group that the estimates are subject to greatest uncertainty. The 'central' projections assume a rise in the birth-rate to the mid-1980s, (associated with the women born in the early 1960s reaching child-bearing age) then falling gradually to the end of the century. If the birth-rate is lower than expected then some savings in social services expenditure, including personal social services, may be expected. Another more general feature of the projections is that the dependency ratio (the ratio of children under 16 plus people of retiring age to the working population), would decrease from 72 : 100 (1974) to 65 : 100 (1986) and remain at levels lower than the present up to the end of the century. This easing of pressure in terms of the proportion of dependent old and young should aid social services in the process of adaptation to changing functions in society.

Specific features with implications for personal social services can be categorised for each age group. Nearly one-third of personal social services expenditure is for children. In the 0–4 age group there is a steady increase in demand over the decade. This has particular implications for day-care and children at risk. Even on lower projections it is unlikely that demand for day-care will be fully met, although a higher proportion of priority needs would be met; local authorities need to monitor birth-rates in their areas closely to identify rising need if it occurs. The effects for children 'at risk' and children in care are less easy to determine as recent decline in the child population has been coupled with increasing numbers of chil-

Table 5. Projected population 1975–2001 (millions)

	0–4	5–15	16–24	25–64	65(60)–74	75–84	85+	65 and over	Total
1975	3.5	9.6	6.9	24.9	6.58	2.22	0.50	9.3	54.2
1980	3.4	9.0	7.6	25.0	6.50	2.49	0.53	9.5	54.5
1985	4.2	8.0	8.1	25.4	6.35	2.71	0.58	9.6	55.0
1990	4.5	8.2	7.5	26.4	6.79	2.79	0.66	9.7	56.3
1996	4.4	9.5	6.4	27.6	6.05	2.69	0.72	9.5	57.4
2001	4.1	9.8	7.0	28.0	5.80	2.74	0.74	9.3	58.2

dren in care. Again, lower variant projections could reduce pressures on child care services, but this factor could be outweighed by increasing incidence of social stress. The main relief from the population factor should come from the decline in the 5–15 age group, which should reach a trough in 1990 and then rise slowly to the end of the decade. For children in care this relief could be partly nullified by increases in delinquency. In the immediate future the potential relief from the lower-variant 0–4 projection and all the 5–15 projections will be balanced by an increase in the 16–24 age group. Unemployment and other social factors are already highlighting the problems of this group which will pose additional problems for personal social services as well as social security, employment, leisure services and housing. The Probation Service is also likely to be affected by this group until the mid-1980s unless changes in the incidence of crime and sentencing policy have a balancing effect. A separate feature of the age groups 0–15 is the higher birth-rate for ethnic minorites. The proportion could increase if the national birth-rate remains very low, with implications for personal social services and also education and housing.

The demographic picture for the elderly is much more certain and in great contrast to the experience of the previous three decades. From 1951–75 the number of elderly rose from 7.6 million to 9.3 million. For the next two decades the total number of elderly shows little variation, but the 75–84 age group increases steadily to 2.8 million in 1990, and remains above 2.5 million to the end of the century. The 85+ group rises from 500,000 in 1975 to 740,000 in 2001. Together the two groups show a total increase from 1975 of 760,000, two-thirds of the increase occurring before 1985. The pressure on personal and social services is likely to be particularly great in the period until 1985 with a gradual levelling off after that. At a time of serious economic constraint it is unlikely that provision will fully match need, and that investment in services will be spaced over the decade. Without additional resources a deterioration in quality and quantity of service for the elderly is very likely until the mid-1980s. Not only do the elderly need a range of domiciliary services and residential care, they form a significant proportion of the chronically sick and handicapped dealt with by social services departments.

Overall the population projections give no certainty about potential reductions in demands for services but some clear evidence of additional demands, particularly from the elderly, the young, and ethnic minorities. The present government has singled out personal

Personal social services

social services as one of the main areas of severe cuts (4 per cent below the level of 1978–79 in 1980–81, thereafter current expenditure increasing at 2 per cent annually to take account of the increase of children in care; capital expenditure to be held level). Whatever its merits or demerits as part of short-term overall economic strategy, the population projections indicate that additional but shifting demands for personal social services will emerge over the next two decades.

Social problems

The incidence of social problems, the second of the demand factors, is notoriously difficult to predict. How a 'social problem' is identified as such and generates a response from social institutions is ill-defined and nebulous. One way of tackling this is to link present patterns of incidence (e.g. of crime) to population levels. This can take us part of the way but even important is to try to delineate some key shifts and trends in social attitudes and behaviour. Many of these are directly or indirectly related to demand for personal social services. A list of trends tending to create individual, family and social stress would include:

(a) relatively high unemployment rates during the next two decades compared to the quarter century after the Second World War;
(b) regional and sub-regional relative economic decline; continuing social problems in conurbations and some rural areas;
(c) geographic mobility in response to structural change, diminishing the capacity for relatives to give and receive family support;
(d) continuing and increasing high rates of divorce;
(e) increasing numbers of single-parent families;
(f) relatively low income, poorer health, and poor housing for several groups – single-parent families, the elderly, the mentally ill, the physically and mentally handicapped, ethnic groups, the unemployed – in fact, all the 'social minorities' described by Peter Townsend in *Poverty*, (Townsend 1979) and analogous to the 'growth outcasts of *Interfutures*';
(g) high or increased crime, aggressive and violent behaviour as a frustration response, social unrest.

Most of these are not new trends, but most show no signs of major abatement and many indications of worsening. Some groups, such as the mentally ill and mentally handicapped, have over a long

Social work 2000

period had fewer resources devoted to their needs than other groups using health and personal social services. In face of the economic pressures of public services these long-term neglected groups face further assaults on their meagre standards of living and quality of life.

Social policy

The third demand factor, social policy in other parts of the Welfare State, concerns the way in which responsibility for dealing with social problems and providing services is allocated between different central and local government departments, with varying degrees of coordination. The Seebohm Report recognised that somewhere in the region of 60 per cent of the work of the separate welfare departments involved some measure of housing and financial need. Work with children and families, the elderly, the mentally ill, and the mentally or physically handicapped also involved close liaison with hospital and community health services. Therefore there are vital liaison and boundary issues with the health service, social security services (particularly the Supplementary Benefits Commission), and local authority housing departments. Along with the probation services, personal social services departments have major links with the police authorities and education departments. Except for the police and probation services, all the other key services are subject to severe financial constraint, arising from static or reduced cash limits. In the short term, it can be reasonably assumed that each service will act defensively, attempting to restrict its resources to its core statutory functions with a limitation on discretion exercised positively towards beneficiaries. Thus the revised 1980 Supplementary Benefits Administration still allows discretion but tries to minimise its role. There will be greater efforts to press families to seek cash or material help from local authorities. Similarly, local authority housing programmes are being seriously curtailed at the same time as expenditure through housing associations is being reduced. The result will be a tendency for social services departments to be coping with more children who are in unsatisfactory home conditions and families defined as not being homeless, but, in fact, having no reasonable accommodation. In addition, plans for small group houses in the community for the mentally ill, and the mentally and physically handicapped, will be seriously affected. Children leaving care and single young-parent families and single adults will find it harder to find accommodation.

Personal social services

In health services there will be less flexibility in the care of the elderly who will be caught between restricted hospital accommodation and static or reduced expenditure on residential care and also domiciliary services. The tendency in hospital administration will be for the shortest possible in-patient period with quick discharge, throwing additional burdens on already stretched home-help and domiciliary medical services. Joint funding projects are likely to remain a marginal contribution to service patterns (£45 m. in 1980–81, 0.005 per cent of health and social services expenditure).

Over recent years, until the Supplementary Benefit Commission was abolished in November 1980, the Supplementary Benefits Commission Annual Reports have recommended greater clarification of functions between the major service providers. Also the Central Policy Review Staff identified poor central and local government coordination of policy and administration as a major obstacle to efficient social service administration, and this was clearly shown in the *Community Development Projects* (Specht 1976). These defects seem likely to worsen in the immediate future.

On the assumptions so far, all three factors of population size and distribution, incidence of social problems, and social policy in other parts of the Welfare State combine to increase demand on personal social services, particularly in the next five to ten years, and remaining relatively high during the following decade. The pressure is uneven, however, and effective monitoring of population and social trends and the regional and sub-regional levels will be essential to anticipate particular areas of demand, establish priorities, and undertake forward planning of staff and physical and financial resources. What are the possible responses to this demand, given that the short-term priority is almost inevitably the protection of service to the most disadvantaged groups, and maintenance of statutory functions?

LONG-TERM STRATEGY

The main response should be firstly to develop a long-term directional strategy, pin-pointing areas of demand and the timing of demand to provide a framework for detailed planning. The second response should be to keep firmly in view the commitment to the shift from institutional care to community care. This part of the strategy is complex, involving not only fewer children in residential care or mentally handicapped in hospitals, but also liaison with health authorities, housing departments and housing associations. In some areas there may be a need for an increase in residential provision, e.g. for the elderly. There is no doubt that this shift could proceed much more rapidly with a range of financial incentives for local authorities and the health services. For instance, resources released by long-term discharge to the community of the mentally ill and handicapped could be shared equally between the local authority, to be used jointly by housing and social services departments, and the health authority, for up-grading care in the hospital setting. The DHSS should take a far more active role in devising financial and administrative machinery for such a transition. A much closer link in finance, planning and provision of accommodation for social need groups is necessary between housing departments and social services departments. The Department of the Environment and the DHSS could do far more in devising administrative and financial incentives to promote such coordination. Financial disincentives to cooperate have been long-standing problems in achieving what every agency wants in theory – good-quality community care.

Other strategies

If these two central foci of a strategy for social services are established, there is still the need to examine complementary response. A key part of this will be the influence on government to restore low to moderate growth levels in the personal social services as the economy regains momentum. This approach does not do away with the necessity to examine the range of other measures which may ensure that welfare needs are met adequately. A greater role for volunteer efforts, private profit-making organisations, and voluntary non-profit-making organisations, are policies which could reduce the need for local authority personal social services provisions

Volunteers

Volunteers are already extensively used in the personal social services, though many commentators argue for a greater extension. The possibility of a net saving to public services depends on the existence of a reservoir of volunteers, the tasks which it is reasonable for volunteers to undertake and which they are willing to undertake, and whether these tasks supplement rather than replace those of paid and trained workers. A library service in a hospital, for example, improves the quality of life for the patients but does not diminish the need for nurses and doctors. In personal social services major uses are for friendly home-visiting and support, providing transport and friendly visits to those in residential care; with children in care there are specific Aunts and Uncles schemes, while most foster-parents are voluntary workers receiving maintenance grants for foster-children. All these are valid and highly desirable forms of voluntary help, but it should be recognised that befriending people who are in dependency relationships can be full of pitfalls and need support from full-time staff. The reservoir of volunteers willing and able to undertake this work may not be limitless. More married women are working (estimated 7.1 million in 1981 and 8.1 million in 1991) and well over 60 per cent of women aged 35–54 are working, higher than in most European countries. It is perhaps from the 16–24 age group and the 55–65 that the most potential for additional involvement lies, although the 60–69 age group already has the highest participation rate in social and voluntary work (11 per cent of the age group). *Social Trends* (1979) indicates that participation rates in social and voluntary work are highest for professional and intermediate non-manual occupations (12 and 13 per cent), indicating perhaps most scope for additional recruiting of skilled and non-skilled manual workers.

Two further points need to be made. There is almost certainly scope for relieving home-helps and social workers of some visiting and practical help functions. But the demands in other areas of work are likely to absorb any time thus relieved. Another point is that volunteer resources need organising and full-time support, whether through independent volunteer bureaux or social work staff; above the line additional expenditure to voluntary agencies or local authorities is involved. Dealing with more difficult situations would require training and additional professional support. Volunteer help, though an important adjunct in the future development of personal social services, will not bring large net savings to public expenditure; at least in the short term they require additional resources to promote development. Any discussion of voluntary help should also take account that participation in voluntary social work is only one of many activities in leisure time, competing with sport, religious practices, trade unions, etc. Families are already the major contributors of voluntary help to the sick, disabled, handicapped and elderly, a fact still insufficiently acknowledged in public discussion.

The present use of volunteers by social workers is fairly modest, and crude estimates have indicated that 13,000 local authority social workers have the help of at least 40,000 volunteers aiding nearly 70,000 clients. The Probation Service may account for a further 10,000 volunteers working in conjunction with 4,000 probation officers. There is no doubt that the use of volunteers in statutory social work services could be extended; the numbers of elderly and mentally and physically handicapped could absorb greatly increased volunteer help over the next two decades. Policy options have been examined in depth by the BASW sponsored study *Social Workers and Volunteers* (Holme and Maizel 1978) but, as has been argued, while the quality of life of those helped would tend to be improved, it would not be with savings to existing services. Whether in supplementary or complementary roles, volunteers extend the range and quality of service without diminishing the overall needs of essential basic services. The Wolfenden *Report of the Committee on the Future of Voluntary Organisations* recognised that generalist intermediary voluntary organisations were essential to mobilising voluntary resources and would need additional finance in the future from central government if an adequate national pattern were to be built up. Some people would argue that a new reservoir of volunteers exists in the army of unemployed although supporters of this view would not put it as crudely as that. In considering this proposition we may ask why social work is singled out rather than voluntary work in defence, education or the police? The answer probably lies in the fact that social workers are not yet as effectively unionised as many workers and so may not resist as strongly as other groups who would be more likely to see 'volunteer' workers as cheap labour, defusing to some extent the demand for jobs and potential civil disorder. Functionally, however, the purpose is the same in social work as in any field of employment, that is, some form of public works activity to keep the unemployed 'usefully' occupied at minimum cost to the State. In recent years the situation has been changing and social workers have shown a stronger interest in union activity; any suggestion which seemed to incorporate voluntary community services as a significant and long-term part of an unemployment package would be likely to meet substantially stronger resistance now than ten years ago. Limited schemes of personal community service of a temporary nature would not meet the same resistance, and in conjunction with the Manpower Services Commission those in personal social services, along with other employment fields, should be imaginative in formulating projects which might otherwise be impossible over the next few years. Even so, the oversight and liaison which such projects involve is an addi-

Personal social services

tional burden on the time of permanent staff and would require additional financial support from central government.

Charities

Extension of voluntary non-profit services is another complementary approach which is sometimes felt could diminish the need for statutory services. Voluntary organisations have always played an important integral role in British social services, and many of these organisations have an impact on statutory personal social services. Some examples are: the national child care organisations such as Dr Barnardo's, the National Children's Home, and the NSPCC; voluntary probation hostels; Richmond Fellowship homes for the mentally ill; homes for physically handicapped children and adults provided by Cheshire Homes and the Spastics Society; Family Service Units; local community organisations and the CAB; play-groups and voluntary youth organisations. These organisations provide a direct service, often to client groups where the existing levels and quality of services is low. Other voluntary organisations maintain a predominantly educational and pressure group role, such as MIND, CPAG, Age Concern.

These organisations with an educational and pressure group role will tend to increase demands on local authority personal social services, as do organisations with advice and information functions. Direct service providing organisations relieve pressure on local authorities in the sense that if they ceased to provide service, there would be greater need for direct provisions; this is particularly so where the total level of provision falls well short of need. What scope is there for further extensions of voluntary organisation direct service? Two features of trends in voluntary provision should be noted. Firstly, an increasing proportion of income has tended to be drawn from local or central government as grants or per capita payments. Donations from individuals to charities have been falling in real terms during the last decade and this appears to be a long-term trend rather than simply a product of inflation. It could have been supposed that increasing real income would lead to greater contributions to charities but the demand for life-styles which include cars, a range of other consumer durables, and more spending on leisure activities including holidays, has outweighed such a possible effect. It may also be true that the general public assumes that contributions through taxes and rates are intended to support adequate public services; statutory social services are thought to be the main community providers. One of the reasons for the expansion of provision in the personal social services field has been the recognition that voluntary services are in general not equipped to provide a universal service. Secondly, the voluntary sector associated with personal social services has largely adopted salaries and service conditions comparable with the statutory sector. Direct service provision is therefore often as expensive as in the statutory sector.

These trends have led to a closer integration of voluntary with statutory provision, making it dependent to a substantial degree upon public finance and meeting objectives agreed with grant providers. It is therefore most unlikely that over the next two decades any major transfer of provision to the voluntary organisations will occur. The reverse, the continuation of present trends, seems far more likely. Many voluntary organisations are now experiencing serious financial difficulty at the same time as central and local government grants and expenditure are being cut back. Any assumption that voluntary organisations will take up the slack from reduced local authority provision is extremely unrealistic. If voluntary organisations are to expand provision they will be largely dependent on central and local government finance or fiscal exemptions; the expansion of the CAB in the mid 1970s and the Volunteer Centre are examples of this kind. It is a fallacy to assume that reduction of State service will inevitably increase voluntary resources. In this context the Wolfenden Committee (Wolfenden Report 1977) has already stated that voluntary expenditure (approx. £1,000 m.) for social and environmental services was equivalent or greater than total State expenditure on personal social services over the past quarter century. Its tenor is that without central government strategic planning for voluntary effort and additional central government support (whether through tax concessions or grants) expansion will be difficult. Reactions to the latest round of spending cuts indicate that this view may have been too optimistic and that the maintenance of present levels of voluntary service will be in jeopardy unless central government supports exhortation with resources. The Wolfenden Committee concluded, *'It is for them (the government) to take, urgently the initiative in working out, with the variety of agencies which are now operating in the field, a collaborative social plan which will make the optimum and maximum use of resources.'*

Profit-making organisations

The other potential area of expansion is private profit-making provision. So far the major form of this provision is of residential care for the elderly and, to a lesser extent, for children. As in education and health a major school of thought, associated with the Institute of Economic Affairs, suggests that 'voucher schemes', coupled with reduced taxation, should enable consumers to choose public or private services. The private residential section for the elderly is similar to the private health and educational sectors in that it caters for the relatively high income groups; it is likely that further development will occur in this field by the linking of insurance and pension plans to private sheltered housing and nursing provision. These are, however, likely to make only marginal impact on overall levels of provision by local authorities and charities. The higher income groups have traditionally used private provision for the elderly and new varieties of scheme may extend the range of provision and introduce a variety of funding arrangements without affecting demand from lower income groups. The private sector, as in health and education, will also not involve itself in provision for those with chronic health and social problems because of the costs.

For other groups besides the elderly – families, the handicapped, chronically sick, deprived children, mentally ill – the scope for private profit-making services is extremely limited. All surveys of the clientele of social services departments show a preponderance of those with low incomes receiving State benefits as their major source of income. These groups are unlikely to provide a market for costly labour-intensive services. Greater profit-making provision as a means of relieving statutory personal social services remains a fantasy rather than a reasonable proposition. It is worth noting that even the marginal additional provision in the care of the elderly is likely to result in increased statutory expenditure in regulating the private sector to avoid abuse and low standards in individual establishments.

Charging for personal social services

If expansion of volunteers, charitable organisations and profit-making organisations is unlikely to relieve demand for statutory personal social services, could charges provide sufficient income to reduce significantly the cost of services or finance extended services? The largest contributions at present come from the payments by the elderly in residential care; these payments are mainly a transfer payment from income maintenance to personal social services. Smaller contributions come from maintenance payments for children in care and for home-help services; these are means-tested.

To make a significant impact these charges would have to be at a much higher rate than at present. However, means-testing – given the low incomes of most clients – would seriously limit the amount of income from this source, whilst deterring many clients in real need from using services. Experience from the health services shows that charges cannot be anything but a subsidiary form of income, without seriously affecting demand. It is probable that use of dental and optician's services by low income groups (adults) is seriously affected by cost factors. A further problem in relying more extensively on charges would be higher administrative costs in means-testing and collecting contributions. Moreover much of the work of personal social services, e.g. in relation to children and families, is at the instigation of the community – referral by police, general practitioners, health visitors, education welfare officers, psychiatrists, supplementary benefits officers. The investigative and visiting work entailed by these referrals could not be charged to clients; similarly many potential users of services have to be persuaded to overcome a reluctance to use services of great potential benefit. As has already been noted, many users of service have financial and housing need as an important part of their situation and could not be charged for work, often time-consuming, in ensuring that maximum use of social security benefits and consideration by the housing departments is achieved.

Ken Judge showed (Judge 1978) clearly that in the field of home-help charges and of charges for nursery places there was a deterrent effect on demand. Experience with prescription charges shows that provided the charge is not too large in absolute terms a fairly sizeable increase has an immediate deterrent effect but grows again to previous levels after a year or so. It has to be remembered that 50–60 per cent of the population is exempt from prescription charges and that a high proportion of personal social clients are in the exempted categories. Thus limited increases in charges for personal social services might have a greater deterrent effect than in the health field, and large increases would certainly cut off many clients from much needed service. It is worth recalling that Ralph Harris and Andrew Seldon, in their *Choice in Welfare* surveys (1971:48) partially explained the opposition and criticism of academics and sceptics by suggesting that they

Are characteristically concerned or preoccupied with the lowest income groups . . . it would appear that even 'people of modest means' are ready to use medical care outside the DHSS in the hope of finding something better, even at personal costs to themselves, provided that they can be given some encouragement or at least partly or wholly absolved from paying for the State service they do not use.

Pensioners and children were excluded from the survey, so it is hardly surprising that the relatively fit working population would like to be relieved of the burden of supporting the old, chronically sick and disabled, and mentally handicapped. It is just this unconcern with the fate of substantial minorities of the population which makes those involved with personal social services cautious in this respect of large shifts to private profit-making welfare and heavy charges. For this reason alone, limited experiments for particular services and in selected areas – as advocated by Harris and Seldon – should not be feared. But until such investigations provide adequate data, our present imperfect knowledge would argue for caution as the potential losses to the most disadvantaged groups in the community need to be weighed against the possible marginal gain to the majority. Pricing social services is a complex subject, partly because of theoretical difficulties and partly because of the paucity of data (e.g. on elasticity of demand). Any cavalier approach to introducing substantial charges on the assumption that deprived groups would be protected by negative income tax would be ignoring the uncertainty of our knowledge and the fact that the effects would be crucially influenced by the level of negative income tax. Were negative income tax to be at a level which reduced the 'social wage' and combined with new or greatly increased charges, resources would be subject to greater maldistribution in relation to need than at present.

SUMMARY AND DISCUSSION

Personal social services expanded considerably in the early 1970s, from a low baseline of provision of some services, and levelled off in the latter part of the decade. The probability of steadily increasing demand is high but will occur in a climate of, at most, moderate national economic growth when public expenditure is under attack. None of the alternatives – volunteers, provision by charities and profit-making organisations, and charging – is likely to reduce significantly the demand for statutory personal social services. The only long-term strategy likely to make an impact on costs is a shift to community care, improved central and local government coordination, and better planning. In the immediate future, planning is

Social work 2000

Table 6

	Social services expenditure (£ m).	% of public expenditure	Personal social services expenditure (£ m.)	% of social services expenditure
1978–79 (out-turn)	42,061	59	1,335	3.3
1979–80 (expected out-turn)	42.983	57	1,380	3.2
1980–81 (plans)	42,465	57	1,289	3.0

(at 1979 Survey prices)
Source: *The Government Expenditure Plans, 1980–81* HMSO, 1979

difficult because of reductions in personal social services expenditure. Planned expenditure 1978–81 was as shown in Table 6.

The government expect that (Cmnd. 7746, 1979).

savings will as far as possible be made by further increases in efficiency, by reducing or eliminating low-priority provision, by developing policies designed to help people to help themselves and others, and by promoting collaboration with the voluntary sectors. Where reductions in standards of provision prove necessary, authorities will be relied on to implement these in ways which protect the most vulnerable. Authorities have also been asked to give priority as far as possible to those services for children which are concerned with the prevention and treatment of delinquency. Joint finance will continue at the planned level.

The analysis so far has argued in the direction that these policy guidelines are unrealistic and inconsistent. Evidence for this is provided by the Personal Social Services Council in its *Cut in Local Authority Spending on Personal Social Services* (1980). The PSSC found:

(a) hopes that public expenditure cuts could be made solely from cutting administrative waste have proved illusory. Reductions in direct services to consumers have been necessary in order to make the required savings;

(b) there is little evidence of any consistent attempt to protect the most vulnerable. Cuts on services to groups whose need is highest and least provided for are sometimes particularly severe;

(c) in some places residential and community services are being simultaneously reduced;

Personal social services

(d) there is danger that the quality of life for people in residential care will decline;
(e) social services departments are likely to concentrate on the fulfilment of statutory obligations, on crisis rather than preventive work, and on high-priority rather than low-priority groups;
(f) creative new approaches to meeting social need are unlikely to prosper, either in the statutory or in the voluntary sector;
(g) strategies for making less immediate effect on consumers have led to short-term savings which may impede long term planning and decrease the efficiency with which scarce resources are used;
(h) the impact of cuts is retrogressive. Traditional modes of care are most resistant to economies. Services which encourage self-help and which represent the enabling role of social services departments are most easily cut;
(i) inequalities in the nature, extent and quality of service provision in different areas will increase as a result of variation in the economics expected of social services departments and in the ways in which these are achieved;
(j) there is little probability that a sufficient expansion and reorganisation of the voluntary sector can be achieved to compensate for reductions in the statutory sector.

When moderate economic growth is re-established, it should be possible to formulate and implement plans and priorities in a more constructive way. But it has already been shown that, for example with the elderly, the next five years are going to place great pressures of demand on services. The priority must be to re-establish a limited growth at least consistent with population change, to meet basic levels of need, and to provide better service for Cinderella groups. Planned personal social services expenditure after 1980–81 is: 1981–82 – £1,310m.; 1982–83 – £1,340m.; 1983–84 – 1, 360m. In the words of Cmnd. 7841, *'This presumes that after a period of retrenchment in 1979–80 and 1980–81 standards will be maintained taking account of demographic change and number of children in care.'* This expectation is almost certainly too optimistic. The rate support allocation 1981–82 will be unlikely to cover inflation costs; without additional increases in rates, there are likely to be further reductions in services in the personal social services sector, i.e. slight increases in expenditure flows will not be reflected in volume increases for services. It is more likely to be 1982–83 before services can allow for expansion, but nevertheless this period must be used to plan in an innovatory way, to be ready for implementation at the earliest moment.

The implication of this broad analysis is that the needs for social services and personal social services will not disappear in the foreseeable future. Limited or only slowly-increasing resources for personal social services must be faced squarely as a challenge where successful adaptation will only occur through innovation in the use of physical and human resources and by cooperation between services.

Chapter four
SOCIAL WORK AND THE WELFARE STATE

As the Welfare State expanded after the Second World War, so the employment of social workers grew. The expansion was particularly fast in the late 1960s and early 1970s after the formation of social services departments in 1971. Training expanded to meet the demand for social workers, with both training and the employment of social workers levelling in the late 1970s. Social work is often taken to be synonymous with social services departments but social workers are only a small proportion of total employees. In England in 1979 there were only 12,930 basic grade social workers; in addition there were 4,932 senior social workers, 534 community workers, 1,048 trainee social workers and 3,288 social work assistants. Field social workers (social workers and senior social workers) accounted for approximately 9 per cent only of a total staff of 193,613. This misconception has led politicians astray. Jo Grimond, writing in 1978 commented:

Unfortunately, a great vested interest in the social services has grown up. Social workers are organising themselves into a profession like lawyers. No doubt like lawyers they will persuade themselves that things can only be done as they always have been done in the way they have been taught to do them. No doubt the disappointing results of their methods will have as little effect as the results of the legal system and its failure to serve the public in a cheap and satisfactory way has had upon lawyers. So their activities will no doubt be extended further.

Grimond's confusion of social work with the whole of personal social services is compounded by false comparison with lawyers. Social workers have, on the whole, had responsibilities placed upon them rather than seeking to extend their orbit of responsibility indefinitely. They have pressed for changes in social policy which if achieved would lessen the need for their services. Also, apart from the negligible group of social workers with a small private practice social workers do not charge for their services and are certainly less well-paid than lawyers. How can it happen that an informed politician can display such ignorance and misunderstanding about social work? It is hardly surprising then that misconceptions abound in the press and public debate. For this reason the earlier sections have dealt with the context in which social work will operate over the next two decades. The present discussion uses this context as a basis for discussing the functions of social work and the shifts which need to be made in response to changing economic and social conditions.

A first pragmatic question is 'Are social workers useful?' It is worth recalling that Clement Attlee had no such doubts when he wrote *'The Social Worker'* in 1920, and Titmuss, in his history of the Second World War describes the increasing demand for social workers as a result of a recognition of their ability to work in a variety of difficult situations, with evacuees, the homeless, servicemen with psychiatric problems, disturbed children. Titmuss (1950) commented that in the wake of personal difficulties thrown up by the war 'the gulf between administrative provision and the actual and effective implementation and use of such provision needed constant bridging; it was the job of social workers to build the bridges'. The starting point is not 'Is social work necessary?' but 'What are the functions which will enable it to play the most positive role in the development of personal social services in the 1980s and 1990s?'

FUNCTIONS OF SOCIAL WORK

Many writers have sub-divided the functions of social workers into complex lists of categories. Such complex divisions of the social work role and task are often more confusing than helpful, and broad categories are sufficient for reasonable debate. The following list has the merit of being brief, but allows further division if necessary:
1. Information and advice (available services, access to services, clarification of straightforward personal or social problems).
2. Assessment of social situation (including formal eligibility for particular services).
3. Facilitating use of service (making practical arrangements, administrative work, liaison with other services).
4. Provision of service (individuals, families, groups and commu-

nity, e.g. family case work, intermediate treatment, initiating self-help groups, working with the mentally ill, elderly and deprived children).
5. Linking and advocacy for clients with other agencies, such as housing, education, social security.

This list deals with the contents of the social worker's day-to-day work. Most social workers spend 20 to 33 per cent of their time with clients; 20 to 33 per cent on travelling; and 33 per cent of their time on administrative work. The proportions vary according to the geographical area served and the agency location (hospital, area team office, child and family centres), but a number of surveys shows broadly similar results. The balance is rather different for social workers in residential settings, who usually spend a higher proportion of time in direct work with clients.

The present-day social workers' function can be expressed diagrammatically, as in Fig. 1.

Client in this context may, as argued by BASW, be taken to mean individual, group, or community. However, given the present way in which responsibilities of local authority social services departments are legally defined and the structure of service, most social work is focused on individuals, families and small groups rather than the community; the small number of community work specialists supports this interpretation and justifies separate discussion later. Similarly residential work lies uneasily within this framework and also is discussed later. This is theoretically out of tune with concepts of integrated service provision, but reflects the present situation of largely disjointed administration and distinctive orientation of residential care. The present functioning of social workers presented in this framework is also consistent with NISW studies by M. Goldberg, which show social workers concerned with assessment, brief service to the majority of clients (often dealing with material/financial problems or limited personal difficulties), and more intensive service to children and families and the mentally ill. These latter groups experience more complex environmental/personal/social difficulty and work with them is underpinned by legislation. Client groups receiving relatively limited social worker service are the physically and mentally handicapped and the elderly (Goldberg and Warburton 1979).

It could be argued that the framework has avoided discussion of values and the ultimate purpose of social work in society, which might be expressed as promoting individual/social well-being and functioning at one extreme and social control at the other. Values

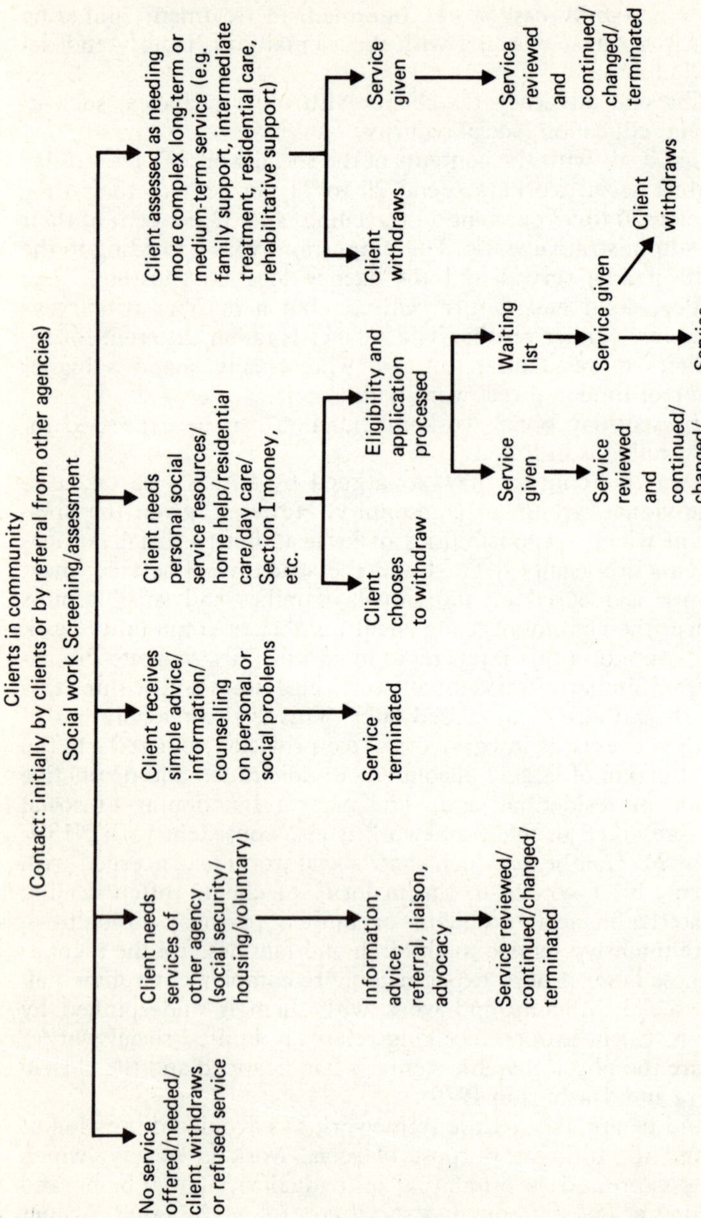

Social work 2000

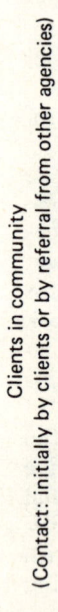

Fig. 1 Social work functions – a flow diagram

Social work and the Welfare State

receive further attention in Chapter 6. This is deliberate. It may be admitted that there are a constellation of values and principles which seem to underpin social work, but these do not seem to be distinctive to the social work profession, sharing much with other professional codes of ethics and also emphasising the rights of citizens in a democracy. However, it would be unrealistic not to acknowledge that in contrast to doctors and teachers who deal with all strata of society, the preponderance of the work of social workers is with groups who are in some way disadvantaged, suffering from environmental, financial and social impoverishment. It is to be expected, and is desirable (though uncomfortable for society at large), that social workers should have a critical view of society and the way in which social problems are generated and dealt with. As Attlee (1920) said:

The social worker must have definite views – must have formed some clear conception of what society he wishes to see produced – and I think it is a mistake for him to hold aloof from reform movements . . . the social worker has as much right to make clear his view as anybody else.

To put it in a different way. Society is denying itself the possibility of much valuable information on the problems of society and the present ways of dealing with them if social workers are constricted in their capacity for informed comment out of direct experience. To describe this sort of critical function as politically perverse or going beyond the proper function of social work is like denying doctors the right to comment on health services or teachers on education. It is their place in the social services and direct experience of those in need, which gives rise to social workers' concern with social reform – not an imagined dogmatic allegiance to left-wing political parties. This myth probably has its origins in the confusion of social workers with sociologists, whose patient research into society and its problems is mostly ignored and Marxist tendencies emphasised. Present penal policies are a classic example of ignoring social science, producing contradictory and ineffective policies. Thus, over and above the day-to-day functions of social workers in the welfare state, they have an essential role in providing information and a critical appraisal of social services (BASW 1970; CCETSW 1980).

THE NEXT TWO DECADES – RELATIONSHIPS WITH OTHER SOCIAL SERVICES

It has already been argued that policy coordination and planning are a priority. Trends suggest that limitations on the growth of the Welfare State will produce an emphasis on core rather than on boundary functions. It is not enough simply to suggest improved coordination and planning. Structures are needed. Two possibilities at central government level which should be explored are:

(a) appointment of a super-Minister for Social Services (housing, education, health, social security, personal social services) as an analogy with the Ministry of Defence. This Minister would have the power to initiate central government coordination and consistency of policy;
(b) appointment of non-departmental junior ministers for children, the elderly, the mentally ill, etc., to ensure, as has to some extent happened with the Minister for the Disabled, that policy for particular groups is consistent across not only social services ministries, but also in taxation and employment.

Both these suggestions would ensure greater coordination between officials through standing and *ad hoc* committees. These central government initiatives should be complemented at the local level by bi-lateral policy coordination between social services departments and medical services, education and housing departments, and social security and unemployment services.

For social workers there are a number of possible changes which could improve liaison, given that the structure of social services is likely to remain complex, with individuals and groups in need using services singly and in a variety of combinations.

1. *Outposting*: appointment of specialist workers in social security, housing, employment, providing service of the type medical social workers provide in general practice and hospitals. The advantages of development in this direction are improvements in referral practice, early screening, and offering of appropriate social work services.
2. *Intake teams*: development of high-quality assessment work combined with brief service. This would be analogous to general practitioner work in medical services.
3. *Specialist assessment/brief service workers in general teams*: as with (2), the main aim of this pattern would be to relieve social workers dealing with more intensive long-standing work systematically.

Each of these approaches would strengthen referral liaison links with other agencies. An important part of this role would be communicating the extent and range of personal social services in an accurate and realistic way.

Social work and the Welfare State

Some relief to personal social services would occur if information and advice services were structured more effectively at a local level. Partnership with CAB or other community-based agencies could serve as the basis for a more generally available and reliable information/advice needs to cover the whole spectrum of social services, i.e. local, national and voluntary agencies, and is more appropriately located in an independent agency, even though substantially financed from statutory funds.

None of these suggestions removes the necessity for all social workers to have a basic grasp of statutory and voluntary benefits and resources appropriate to different kinds of need. The rationale is more directed to efficiency to service; a strong volunteer component is feasible provided that there is a full-time organisational presence and professional supporting staff.

A further issue is the development of quasi-social work functions in other social services. Examples are school counsellors and community psychiatric nurses. It was to be expected that health and education services should gradually incorporate approaches which recognised the social dimension of the lives of school-children and the mentally ill and the way it impinges on ability to use education and health service. Community orientations have developed independently in education and health services as well as personal social services. For these reasons it will be important to clarify acceptable areas of overlap and also areas of unproductive duplication. Out-posting and specialists' liaison posts would have important contributions to make. The object should be to avoid wasteful duplication of service. Community psychiatric nurses have grown rapidly in number in the last decade, yet some of the major problem areas for the mentally ill are financial and in finding accommodation and employment; these are areas of work which many community psychiatric nurses are unhappy about dealing with, often referring cases to social workers for their help. There is a case for mental health teams involving both social workers and community psychiatric nurses where appropriate patterns of cooperation which avoid unnecessary duplicated visiting can be developed. This is already in progress in many areas but needs systematic development. As with health visitors, it is important to establish how much of the social work/counselling dimension can be handled within the core role and when referral to personal social services is appropriate.

Social workers' relationships with other agencies are not always comfortable. Where clients are having problems in their relationships with social security and housing departments, social workers may be involved in mediation and advocacy. Social workers can be effective in this role as shown by their work with supplementary benefits tribunals. Because a high proportion of clients is receiving benefits it is essential that welfare rights information and support should be available. The complexity of the welfare system requires that all social workers should be familiar with the most widely used benefits, and be able to inform clients of these. There is also need for access to more expert welfare rights service, whether this is provided by the social services department or by local community agencies.

The whole sphere of relationships with other welfare agencies requires a high degree of skill in written and verbal communication, formal as well as informal structures for liaison and coordination, and administrative expertise. Assisting clients to use available services has always been, and will continue to be, a core function of social work. Continuing trends in selectivity in operating social services, and the tendency for groups of 'social minorities' or 'growth outcasts', will keep this function to the forefront. Training in administration and welfare rights should therefore be accorded a higher priority than hitherto on social work courses.

A simple model (not to exact scale) which shows the importance of relationships with other services would be as shown in Fig. 2.

For families with children and young people, key relationships with other services are:

Health services
Income maintenance
Police and penal system
Housing
Education
Voluntary child care agencies
Probation service.

For the mentally ill, relationships with other services are:

Health services
Police
Employment
Housing
Income maintenance
Voluntary mental health organisations.

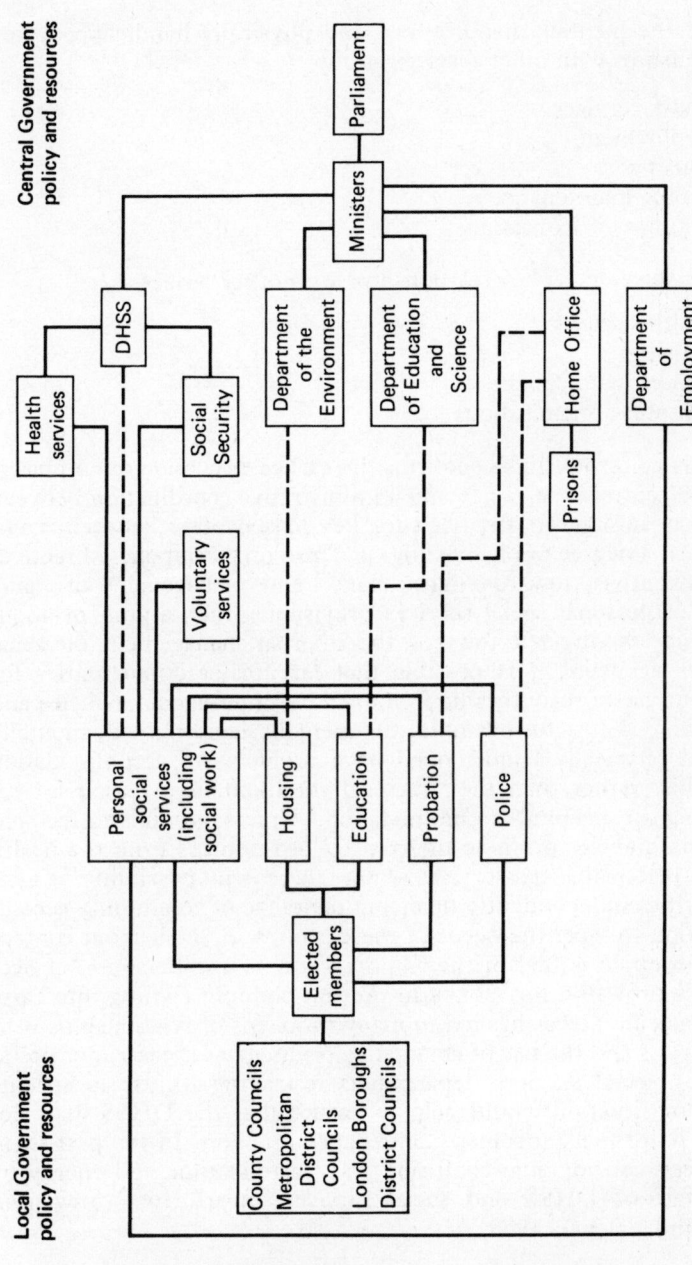

Fig. 2 Links between other social services and personal social services

For the mentally handicapped and physically handicapped, key relationships with other services are:

Health services
Employment
Housing
Income maintenance
Voluntary organisations.

For the elderly, key relationships with other services are:

Health services
Housing
Income maintenance
Voluntary organisations.

This pattern of links confirms the earlier discussion of emphasising the centrality of policy and administrative coordination between services. It suggests the need for key liaison posts between major services, a degree of out-posting, and also financial/policy directives and incentives towards joint finance and management of many types of personal social services provision. Much argument about efficiency is directed towards the internal management of social welfare agencies; it is possible that far greater opportunities for efficient use of resources lie in the field of inter-agency policies and provision. Thus, for example, the mentally handicapped, mentally ill and physically handicapped have problems of accommodation and this, rather than their medical condition, is a reason for remaining in hospital accommodation. Unless administrative and financial policies promote the transfer of resources from the health to the personal social services sector, there is no possibility of local authorities independently financing the range of community accommodation to meet the needs of these groups. A smaller but contentious example is that of the Children and Young Persons Act Section 1's provision for money to prevent children coming into care. This specific power has led to many problems of relationships with the DHSS and the use of emergency payments; a clearer interpretation by social services departments restricting its use to specific types of situation would help to ensure that the DHSS does not avoid its primary incomes maintenance function. In the past there has been considerable confusion and waste of time and energy by the staff of DHSS and social services departments (Stevenson 1973 and Valencia 1979).

A final example is that of intermediate treatment. At present social services departments, the Probation Service, education departments and the police each provide intermediate treatment or an analogous type of service (PSSC 1977). In terms of the main aim of preventing delinquency, such efforts should be coordinated effectively to provide a range of service without undue duplication. Without going into further examples, the principle of effective coordination and finance of joint policy and provision is essential if the role of social workers is not to remain problematical. One of the main reasons for disquiet about the roles and tasks of social workers is the shifting relationships and pressures of other social services. Without firm action in this area the confusions and ambiguities will remain, whatever theoretically neat range of tasks and skills is set out in abstract form.

That central government is slowly beginning to learn these lessons is illustrated by the DHSS Consultative Document *Care In the Community* (DHSS 1981) which followed the publication of *Care in Action: A Handbook of Policies and Priorities for the Health and Personal Social Services* (HMSO 1981). Concerned with the process of moving resources from the health services to local authorities and from institutional health provision to community health provision, the Consultative Document invites comment on the following measures for achieving these aims:

1. Extension of joint finance arrangements.
2. Lump sum or annual payment.
3. Transfer of hospital buildings.
4. Pooling funds for a client group.
5. Central transfer of funds.
6. Earmarking NHS funds.
7. Concentrating responsibility for a client group.

All these suggestions are capable of contributing to an extension of community care. But the Consultative Document envisages that shift of resources must occur without any addition to total resources for health and personal social services, and appears unduly tentative in its view of the DHSS role. The general disposition of strict cash limits in the health service and the plans to severely restrict local government financial freedom in 1982 are not good omens for a positive approach from health services and local government. Taken together with a naïve view that ignores the possibility of short-term additional costs in transferring resources and totally inadequate attention to manpower and training implications, these suggestions are unlikely to yield the rapid change which is required and indicate a lack of firm resolve to implement policy. In spite of all these resolutions, the Consultative Document is to be welcomed for pointing in the right direction and establishing an agenda for action.

Chapter five
SOCIAL WORK METHODS AND PRACTICE

BACKGROUND

The functions of social services departments are set out in the Local Authorities Social Services Act 1970, which lists all the Acts sanctioning the provision of service and giving authority for action by its employees. Particular Acts cover a wide variety of services directed to the welfare of various community groups. Within the legislation there are Acts which emphasise community provision (Mental Health Act 1959; Children and Young Persons Acts 1963 and 1969), but which also give authority to remove children and adults from the community if they are in serious danger or if the community needs protection from them. Preventive work and promotion of welfare receive some specific mention, but there is no general legal power to promote the welfare of the community in England and Wales as is expressed in Section 12 of the Social Work (Scotland) Act 1968. Nevertheless the general climate in Scotland and England and Wales is very similar. Three broad functions cover the work of the departments, and voluntary agencies also have to work within the legal framework and are strongly influenced by the dominant social philosophies in the development of services:
(a) prevention and promotion of welfare; avoiding the need for intensive service;
(b) provision of a wide range of service to those in need and those vulnerable, including residential, day-care, and domiciliary services;
(c) statutory removal of individuals from the community who are a serious danger to themselves or others.

These functions provide the basis for the tension between enabling and controlling, promoting freedom and restricting freedom which social workers, with others, are often having to resolve in practice. Deciding to admit compulsorily the mentally ill or deprived children (more rarely the elderly) to care, demands sensitivity, knowledge and judgement of a high order. Such decisions are also influenced by the climate of public opinion and the availability of a range of community and residential resources.

Another feature of the legislative base for statutory social work is that it lays down in some detail the help to be made available. Legislation in education and health mainly concerns itself with the broad administrative and financial arrangements, without reference to specific medical techniques or teaching methods. In social work, legislation prescribes certain methods and provision as the most desirable, or gives a local authority the duty to provide specific services, while having little to say about the quantity or quality of service needed. Examples of this are intermediate treatment, fostering, adoption. In medicine and education the practitioner is left to decide the methods he will use according to the best professional knowledge and judgement available. Social workers, in contrast, have many of their methods of practice detailed for them in legislation.

This framework within which social workers operate reflects some features of social work which distinguish it from education or medicine in the helping professions, and have to be kept in mind when discussing the detailed methods of social workers. Social work, unlike medicine and education, is not yet categorised as a mainly technical task for experts. Doctors and teachers (and also lawyers) have generally taken strongly defensive positions when the community has tried to influence their practice; there are signs that more doctors and teachers are beginning to support public participation and influence on their practices and methods of deciding priorities. Social work is rightly more responsive to the community in that an outlook which viewed human relationships solely as a technical expertise, will be morally unjustifiable. However the fact that over the next two decades – with an emphasis on economic and materialist values which shows no sign of waning – a high proportion of the clientele will be of disadvantaged groups, will entail a period of inevitable clash and negotiation between the values and interests of minorities and the disadvantaged and those of the majority of the community. Undoubtedly great skills in communication are required of social workers, but the ability to engage constructively in a myriad of detailed transactions with and on behalf of clients demands as much in terms of moral analysis and sensitive judgement. Social workers would be failing in their duty if they did not expose these moral dilemmas to the community at large, partly in an educative role facing the latter with the consequences of its actions, or its inaction. The need for structural change within the economy has been described. This should be to the long-term benefit of the whole community, but in the short and medium term, one of the roles of personal social services and of social workers will be to protect the weak and vulnerable against adverse consequences of economic development; this is likely to be critical during the next decade.

Before examining in more detail methods of working, it is necessary to point out common criticisms of social workers and social services departments. Many of these are presented in *Can Social Work Survive* (Brewer and Lait 1980). A short list might run as follows:
(a) lack of knowledge, e.g. of law or procedures, or of applications to client groups;
(b) lack of experience, e.g. of working with particular client groups, or using particular methods;
(c) a soft or woolly approach by social workers;
(d) a radical or left-wing ideology;
(e) bureaucracy – social workers being too rigid in application of rules and regulations;
(f) social workers offering inappropriate service, e.g. offering casework when clients have asked for material/financial help;
(g) lack of continuity in social work staff.

These criticisms emanate from a variety of sources. Psychiatrists complain of the lack of mental health knowledge or of specialist workers. Directors of social services complain of newly trained workers with poor knowledge of procedures and legislation. Newly trained workers may disagree with departmental policies. Right-wing politicians may regard social workers as soft liberals bailing out inadequate and anti-social elements in the community; social workers may even be lumped with sociologists as left-wing Marxist radicals, part of the alleged Marxist conspiracy in higher education identified by Professor Gould. Clients sometimes complain about bureaucracy, about inappropriate service, or lack of continuity (Rees 1978).

Some of these criticisms are closely related to social work training which will be discussed in a later section. It should be noted that for the most part clients seem generally satisfied with the way in which social workers do their jobs.

A national poll in 1981 (Weir 1981) showed that social workers have a 'good and fairly strong public image'. The survey revealed that:

they are widely regarded as workers who give advice and help to people in difficulties, and especially when children or old people are involved: and that given a choice between a variety of alternative descriptions, people are many times more likely to regard them as: 'caring people in a difficult job' (48 per cent of respondents) than 'soft-hearted do-gooders' (7 per cent), 'a sop to society's conscience[1] (6 per cent) or 'long-haired revolutionaries' (2 per cent)

Similarly, the work that social workers undertake is necessary. During a social work strike in Tower Hamlets in 1978–79, whilst some clients with minor difficulties were able to cope without social work assistance (DHSS 1979):

there was a large number of people who needed the help of good social work during the industrial action and did not get it. The experience of the emergency also showed that the social workers occupied a key position in the Department in contributing to major decisions about the lives of individual clients and to the effective use of departmental resources.

None of the other criticisms is unique to social work except, perhaps, the ideological accusations of liberal softness or left-wing commitment, neither of which is usually supported by evidence of attitudes and political allegiance of social workers. Imperfect knowledge and skills, bureaucracy, lack of continuity of staff, inappropriate methods are also regularly levelled in education and medicine, representing on the one hand the problems of coping with perpetual advances in knowledge, and on the other hand the administrative problems of large organisations employing professionals. Problems of knowledge are rather more acute in social work because of the nature of social work with its special mix of technical and moral dilemmas in social situations, and because of the shorter training for social work and larger proportion of untrained staff. Yet in this area as well as that of other criticisms it is difficult to avoid the conclusion that any problems which social workers experience are generated as much from external conflicting expectations as well as from demonstrable difficulties which any large welfare organisation must face. There is a much better chance that these pressures will be coped with constructively if they are not viewed as uniquely inherent in social work.

ASSESSMENT

Use of any particular method singly or in combination presupposes assessment of situations, whether of individuals, families, small groups or communities. Three stages can be distinguished – involvement in the situation through referral, client's own approach or anticipatory investigation; observation and analysis of the situation; joint definition of the problem with the client leading to proposed action. The participatory nature of the assessment has involved a major shift in the last two decades; it is no longer valid to assume that potential clients are passive objects for objective analysis, using an outdated medical model which is being questioned by doctors themselves. An essential component of the involvement in situations is a recognition that, say, the need for community work services cannot be assessed without a prior knowledge of how that community works. In assessing individual and family situations, how they connect with the local neighbourhood and community is an important focus. Therefore an integral part of any assessment process is the knowledge and understanding by individual social workers and teams of social workers of local communities, their structures, needs and resources. Only where this is adequate can sound decisions be made about the need for additional service and resources provided by personal social services. Shared or joint assessment involving potential clients as well as social workers and other welfare professionals assumes to a greater extent than hitherto the possible withdrawal from service by the clients, decision by social workers not to intervene and, where there is need for service, joint responsibility between client and worker in the implementation of service.

The drive for participation and involvement is likely to develop further during the next decades. It is a reflection of general trends in the community and attitudes to welfare, but is also reflected in professional concepts of 'contract' (used in a general rather than legal sense), between clients and workers as a means of negotiating appropriate service. This position lies uneasily in the framework of local government administration where, in contrast to the medical model, assessment is formulated in terms of bureaucratic eligibility for service. If the aim of social services departments is to adopt greater participation in assessing and negotiating service, making full use of local community resources, there will be a need to develop flexible patterns of administration to enable assessment of need for service and provision to be articulated in a more open-ended way. Participation challenges the lack of resources and weighting of priorities. Inevitably there will be conflicts of interest between elected representatives, different user groups in the community and social services departments. Social workers occupy a central position in mediating and trying to resolve competing claims and relating these conflicts to a professional assessment role. Facing such conflicts calls for both skill and the courage not 'to duck' or fudge issues.

The British Association of Social Workers in *The Social Work Task* (BASW 1977) and the Birch Report (HMSO 1976) both identify assessment as a key function and method of social workers. It involves extensive knowledge of the aetiology and predisposing conditions for social and personal distress using the psychological and social sciences, personal experience of deprived environments and the people exposed to them, and a firm grasp of a wide range of social service and community resources, guided by clear understanding of the legislative basis for intervention. Social workers have to be skilled in not only assessment work but also communicating this verbally and in writing. They must too be aware of any formal criteria which govern eligibility for service and application procedures. All social workers are involved in general assessment work in the community but may also draw on specialist social workers, psychologists or psychiatrists in some complex cases. The importance of the first-line assessment by general social workers or by social workers in intake terms should not be undervalued. In the past, social workers were trained mainly in the use of casework with individuals and families and were more likely to undertake assessment from the stance of deciding whether clients needed casework or not, tending to assume that if there was need for service then casework was the appropriate form of help. This approach is no longer valid. In outlining the functions of social workers assessment was considered a major function alongside the direct provision of service. Such a trend in thinking and practice is vital if potential users of personal social services are to have access to services and their choice maximised.

INTEGRATED METHODS

The preceding discussion of assessment is consistent with what has become known as an 'integrated methods' approach to social work practice (Specht and Vickery 1977). Whereas until the early 1970s work with individuals and families (and, to a lesser extent, small groups) had been the main method of social work taught and used by social workers – loosely described as casework – now most social workers receive teaching which relates to the use of small groups and community approaches as well. The direction of thinking has

Social work methods and practice

been that most social workers should be able to undertake a wider range of methods and so respond more flexibly and appropriately to a range of need in the community. This aim has been imperfectly realised because of the limited opportunities to practice with small groups, and to work with communities during training, and by virtue of the fact that the dominant style of service in social services departments still remains work with individuals and families. Some departments have appointed community work specialists and to a lesser extent group specialists; however the dominant impression is that most basic-grade social workers rely heavily on individual and family methods associated with casework. So a prime aim during the coming years is to broaden the range of service offered by most social workers coupled with a growth of specialist practitioner appointments in group and community work. Because of the existence of a variety of voluntary community work agencies and the existence of community work courses in the youth and community field, social services departments have failed to examine systematically the implications of a wider range of methods, particularly community work, being employed by social workers.

For convenience, some brief comments will be made about particular methods used by social workers; for a more detailed account of social work practice and methods *The Essential Social Worker* (Davies 1981) provides a good introduction and useful bibliography.

1. *Giving information and advice* Given the present imperfect state of information and advice services, social workers should continue to maintain this as a method of working. If adequate general advice and information services were structured in each local authority, this method would be used less by social workers. In the present haphazard organisation and administration of information and advice services, social workers are still a major provider, both giving simple information and advice and referring to specialist agencies in this field. The complex structure of our welfare services still leaves the general public confused, and social workers form one of the main groups of professionals with a sound knowledge of the system. Giving advice and information can be linked organisationally to community work methods and/or to straightforward counselling services. Voluntary workers (already involved in the CAB, for example) can play an increasing part in providing this service.

2. *Simple counselling* There are a variety of voluntary agencies

offering limited counselling and many workers in other social services may offer straightforward personal counselling. Such counselling usually involves the capacity to listen while someone talks about his situation or problems, and clarification aided by the counsellor. Being able to unburden oneself and in the process clarifying the situation is a positive help to many people. Often one or two contacts with the counsellor provide sufficient relief and assistance for people to cope for themselves. The social situation during the next two decades is likely to see an increased need for this type of counselling, and social workers provide this service to many people who approach social services departments, or who are referred there by other agencies. Volunteers can be trained to extend this type of service, but inevitably, it will remain a method used by social workers, in much the same way as a G.P. works with many patients or refers to a social worker when the need is not medical, but social, as when dealing with people under stress in their working or home life.

3. *Mobilising resources and facilitating the use of service* A high proportion of the clients of social services departments are not emotionally disturbed or pathological in their social functioning. They may have physical handicaps, be socially isolated, lack financial resources, need to go into hospital. All these situations may produce stress for individuals and families but associated with this is a need for practical service – home-help assistance, transport, use of a day centre, voluntary visiting, care of children whilst a mother is in hospital. The social worker's method is to examine the range of resources in the community and provided by the social services department and with the client come to decisions about the appropriate services, facilitating their use by using skills in administration and liaison with these services, personalising their use by the particular client. Humane administration, allowing for choice and recognising the worries clients have about their situation and using services, is an essential part of service provision. Assisting people to use appropriate services is not simply an official, bureaucratic, method – which in the past has deterred people from using services and created feelings of guilt and stigma – but one blending personal care and sensitivity with administrative efficiency. Much of this work is indirect and accounts for the large amount of time spent by social workers on administration. Administrative method combined with personal care and service will and should remain a major way of working for social workers. Some of this type of work could be

undertaken by social work assistants or aides under the supervision of social workers.

4. *Complex counselling/casework with individuals* This method is most often used in dealing with families with young children or adolescents and with the mentally ill and their families. The major developments in the last decade have been the growing interest in and the use of family therapy and transactional analysis, coupled with a trend towards brief treatment of three to six months, after which there is an evaluation leading to completion of service or establishment of a new 'contract' of service. The emphasis on clear objectives which can be evaluated is positive, and the approaches can be adapted to work with more chronic longstanding problems, entailing regular review of the objectives and focus of work for limited periods. Use of these methods requires trained social work staff, particularly when it is not possible to use these methods without consideration of other methods as well. This cluster of methods is a key part of the social worker's range of working approaches (sometimes in conjunction with psychologists or psychiatrists) underpinned by behavioural learning theory and psychoanalytic theory. However, because of the apparent technical base and need of professional expertise, it would be retrograde to regard this cluster of methods as the most important rather than as an equal partner to be used where relevant. Identification of social work methods solely with counselling/casework methods would be damaging to the long-term quality of service to the community.

5. *Social group work* Group work also encompasses a cluster of approaches ranging from discussion, educational and activity groups to therapy groups. Activation of community and self-help groups could also be included in the cluster. Use of group methods is very patchy at present. Present applications are day-care groups, groups for adolescents, foster-parents, adoption applicants, rehabilitated people from mental hospitals, patients with particular diseases, delinquents. The use of groups has great potential but needs resources of space and time; many social services departments have inadequate space and facilities, and social workers hard-pressed with a statutory case load and bombarded with referrals may not find the necessary time to use group work systematically. At the moment, therefore, use of groups largely depends upon the initiative of individual social workers, rather than being a structured part of service provision. It is as though a surgeon were expected to per-

form operations without an operating theatre. As with casework/counselling much clearer definition of the client situation where the approach is most likely to be appropriate is required so that group service can be structured in the agency. The aim is not so much savings of time (there are no clear indications that group service is less costly in time and resources than individual service) but more effective service.

6. *Community work* Again this is a hybrid method. Community planning and development, activation of neighbourhood networks and organisations, liaison with local voluntary organisations, establishing neighbourhood centres, would all be included. There may be some limits to social workers using community work methods if they are associated with extreme conflict between community organisations and the local authority. However, whether through direct service by social workers, or through social workers in liaison with voluntary community organisations, social services departments have hardly begun to use this approach fully. This is partly because of the local government structure, which discourages participation and is hypersensitive about criticisms because of the vested interests of officers and elected members. There are signs that there is a growing community orientation and responsiveness to pressures for participation. Realisation is slowly growing that community work may mobilise untapped resources and also give a vital stimulation to the ways in which services are structured and used. The development of community work and a community orientation depends greatly on decisions about how services are structured and managed, and presents social services departments with their greatest challenge over the next two decades.

7. *Advocacy and mediation* Many clients of social services departments, probation departments and voluntary agencies, experience great difficulty in their dealings with social security offices and housing departments, the courts and social services departments themselves. Often basic rights to entitlement are in question, or discretionary decisions. Social workers in this context need to use the methods of mediating between the client and the service in question, or, acting as advocate, help a client to present his situation as clearly as possible, or present it for him. This involves some degree of conflict with other services, but nonetheless is essential if the client wishes to pursue the issue, e.g. in appealing to a supplementary benefits tribunal. Even if the social worker is uncertain

Social work methods and practice

of the outcome or justice of the client's disagreement, the client has the right to use such methods of complaint, appeal or representation as are available. If the dispute is with the social services department, the social worker has the duty to advise his client about the alternative representation if the social worker is a party to the dispute.

THE BALANCE OF FUNCTIONS – CHANGING PRIORITIES

The tasks performed by social workers are complex. At one level they can be described in terms of the broad functions of social work in relation to society and the welfare system. These derive from the need to alleviate the effects of social and economic change, protecting vulnerable individuals, protecting society from individuals who out-step a variety of normative rules (e.g. serious violence or delinquency), promoting constructive social and community development. Such broad functions find expression in the legal and constitutional framework of statutory and voluntary agencies. At the next level tasks are undertaken by social workers in relation to situations and problems involving particular individuals, groups and communities. This is the context within which social workers use assessment skills and the range of methods just outlined. The Birch Report identified areas of work in which social work skills were essential: in circumstances involving loss of liberty or change of home for the clients, compulsorily or voluntarily; in situations demanding the exercise of treatment skills by a qualified social worker or field residential- or day-care settings; in situations demanding complex assessment or treatment planning. The British Association of Social Workers, in *The Social Work Task*, also described roles whose performance depended on a trained social worker; diagnostician; planner; counsellor; attitude/behaviour changer; consultant; implementer and coordinator of plans of action. In both the Birch Report and *The Social Work Task* there is a considerable overlap and measure of agreement with the present outline although they do not give as much weight to the social work involved in relation with other agencies and to facilitating the use of the range of resources in personal social services, other welfare agencies and the community. Given that social workers may spend up to a third of their time in various types of administrative activity (telephoning, writing reports or letters, completing forms), to communicate with clients, colleagues or staff in other agencies, it is noticeable that it is often not regarded as a professional task, or is viewed as a necessary evil. The view taken here is that a much more equal balance of administrative and relationship skills is needed to match the needs of clients with the resource systems of community, personal social service agencies and other welfare services. Personal social service functions inadequately without a framework of humane and sensitive administration. The relationship between the different levels can be put diagrammatically, as in Fig. 3.

Figure 3 shows the scope for conflict and different interpretations of the functions and tasks of social workers. In a pluralistic rather than consensus society the many differing perspectives on the working of society, social problems and how to deal with them are reflected in conflicting emphasis given to the range of tasks which social workers perform. Politicians and the community at large may tend to emphasise direct services to clients and avoidance of social disruption, and to give less weight to the therapeutic functions of social workers and to the conflict/advocacy functions with other agencies. For social workers to take the strain of social malfunctioning is far cheaper and more comfortable than changing social instituitons, challenging vested interests and reducing inequitable income distribution. Education and training institutions are more likely to emphasise the broad purposes of social workers, their methods and their contribution to social reform. Agencies (particularly elected members and management staff) emphasise their formal responsibilities and respond to public and political opinion about interpretation of their functions. Social workers, with a variety of possible functions and methods, have somehow to reconcile all these frequently conflicting influences and expectations in their day-to-day work.

It follows that there is no absolute, unchanging list of functions and tasks with prescribed weightings which would be universally

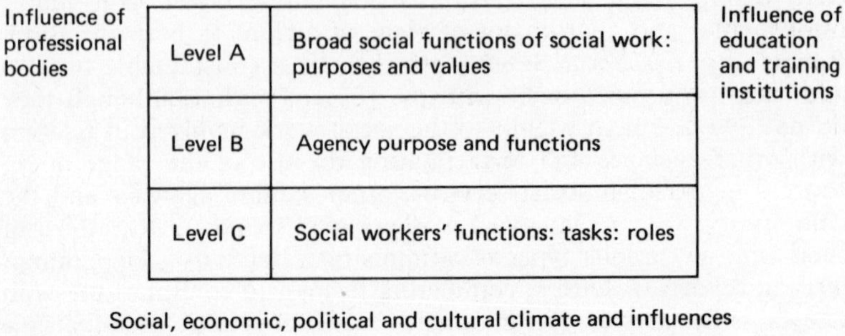

Influence of professional bodies			Influence of education and training institutions
	Level A	Broad social functions of social work: purposes and values	
	Level B	Agency purpose and functions	
	Level C	Social workers' functions: tasks: roles	

Social, economic, political and cultural climate and influences

Fig. 3

Social work methods and practice

acceptable. The tasks and weightings are worked out in processes of conflict, accommodation, and compromise. This situation could lead to a counsel of despair. There is, however, a partial way out of the impasse, namely, identification of some core functions and tasks (on the basis of analysis of the social context) which need greater prominence in the future. Several suggest themselves from the present analyses:

(a) functions and tasks in relation to the access to and use of other welfare agencies, including advocacy, mobilising resources, advice and information, coordination and joint service provision;
(b) functions and tasks in relation to community work and participation;
(c) functions and tasks in the methods areas of complex counselling and social group work:
(d) administration:
(e) assessment;
(f) functions and tasks in supervising and supporting ancillary staff and volunteers.

A different analysis of personal social services would produce a somewhat different list. This interpretation has the merit of not mirroring exclusively the interests of trainers, agencies or politicians, being grounded in what we know of kinds of demands made now and likely to be made in the future. To this list should be added:

(g) functions and tasks in relation to residential care.

Residential care uses about half of the resources of social services departments and merits separate discussion in the next section.

RESIDENTIAL CARE

Until the dissolution of the Poor Law in 1948, residential care had been the main form of personal social service. Since then there has been a consistent trend towards the development of day-care and community forms of service. In child care services this was marked by the development of fostering and adoption services. With the mentally ill it took the form of community hostels; with the mentally handicapped, the development of day centres and training centres. For the elderly, sheltered housing, day centres, and the home-help service have been the main forms of non-residential provision. For the elderly, mentally and physically handicapped and the mentally ill these developments have been associated with reduced numbers of hospital beds and/or shorter stays in hospital. As noted earlier, so far these shifts have not released sufficient resources for community provision in spite of limited joint financing. For some of the groups voluntary community provision is a substantial adjunct to statutory community services.

Simultaneously the purposes and functioning of residential provision has been gradually transformed. Major trends have been the move to smaller units or sub-divided units within larger establishments, improvements in the physical of provision, limited improvements in staffing ratios and training; greater emphasis on treatment as well as care, and moves to develop greater participation by residents. These developments have spread unevenly in provision for different groups and are still in progress.

Implications for the functions and tasks of residential social workers and field social workers stem from these advances. Residential social workers, as well as providing direct caring, have the possibility of using the range of methods which in the past have been mainly associated with fieldworkers. The relevance of the full range of methods is determined by the aims and function of the particular establishment, the ability of staff to employ them and agency practice conventions. A realisation of such potential in the range of service which could be offered has stimulated thinking about innovatory service provision. The concept of the key worker, permitting residential as well as field social workers to have the full responsibility for planning, implementing and coordinating service for a resident is one such development. Another valuable concept is of the residential establishment as a community resource centre. Implementation as yet is very patchy, but the concepts are important contributions to breaking down the frequently sharp division between residential and community provision and improving the quality of service at admission, whilst in residence and on discharge.

At present the form of service is still mainly for residential staff to have day-to-day responsibility for care and treatment within an establishment and for field social workers to have responsibility for planning and coordinating implementation. It is important to recognise that much of the impetus towards the key worker concept comes from the patchy and often tenuous service provided by field social workers. In theory the key functions of field social workers in relation to residential care are: community assessment; joint management of admission with residents and residential staff; continuing contact and service to residents and maintaining links with family and the community; rehabilitation work and preparation in

Social work methods and practice

the community; joint management of discharges; support during the post-discharge period of adjustment. In practice, quality of admission and continuing service after admission is frequently weak and erratic, particularly with the elderly and mentally handicapped. There is also evidence, for example with delinquent children, that at the assessment stage, some social workers are too ready to recommend residential care as a preferred form of care, sometimes as a response to public attitudes.

Thus, for the future, certain key elements stand out as requiring urgent attention. Underlying all the elements is the need to understand better the relationship of the individual to the institution and to change attitudes as well as the use of resources.

(a) strengthening of community assessment by field social workers where residential care is a possibility;
(b) reviewing and, where necessary, changing or extending the functions of residential establishments;
(c) extending the range of functions and methods of residential social work staff either in line with the flexible key-worker pattern, or as a general pattern for residential social work staff;
(d) great emphasis on quality of admission work;
(e) greater priority to rehabilitation work;
(f) strengthening discharge and post-discharge support work;
(g) developing greater participation by residents in the management of the establishment and in decision-making in their own lives;
(h) more systematic use of individual counselling internal and formal groupwork and community involvement.

It is easier to pinpoint the areas for future development than to structure the use of staff resources to meet these aims. The Birch Report recommends that there should be at least one CQSW trained member of staff in each establishment, is far from realisation. In the medium term it could be that the way to make progress is to designate key posts in residential establishments with some of the above functions and to use staff development resources. Alternatively, staged plans for individual establishments or groups of establishments could be introduced. One of the features of developments in residential care is that changing concepts of practice have developed much faster than the ability of staff to reorient attitudes and practice. Desired improvements have outpaced the capacity of training resources in educational establishments and agencies to prepare and equip staff for changed functions and roles. Therefore to the list (a) to (h) above, should be added:

(i) increased priority for training residential social work staff and day-care staff; devising forms of part-time or modular training which would enable greater access to training opportunities.

Many of the developments for residential apply also to day-care establishments. Broadening their functions, using a wider range of methods, and acting as a community-based resource centre, indicate the general directions of change. Already progress is being made in provision of day/residential care from the same centre. Both residential care and day-care are group forms of provision and as such should be centres where specialised group service is developed systematically.

CLIENT GROUPS

Different client groups make differential use of services and also receive service from different types of worker. The mentally ill and families with children in long-term contact with the social services departments are more likely to be dealt with by qualified social workers, in contrast to the elderly, the mentally handicapped and physically handicapped where a higher proportion of clients are dealt with by unqualified social workers, or social work assistants. It could be assumed that this is because they need more practical help than other groups. The Goldberg and Warburton study (1979) shows clearly, however, that for almost all client groups approximately half were in receipt of some form of practical help, the type of practical help varying according to age and problems. (The visually handicapped were exceptional in that over 90 per cent of clients received some form of practical help.) Similarly between one-quarter and two-fifths of clients received services such as information and advice, and mobilising resources. Perhaps the most significant difference was that the physically and the mentally handicapped received less review visiting than the elderly, children and families and the mentally ill, a reflection of statutory requirements in the case of children, and of public attitudes and expectations in the case of the elderly and the mentally ill. In general then, the greater use of staff other than qualified social workers did not seem to depend on the nature of the problems of clients but upon a differential and at times arbitrary perception of need and priorities.

It is obvious from statistics on the use of all staff of social services and the distribution of resources that the physically and the mentally handicapped and the mentally ill receive the least service. Large absolute increases in services obscure the low level of service

Social work methods and practice

before the Seebohm reorganisation. A major effort will be needed in the next two decades to ensure that these groups receive a fairer share of resources. This should be achieved by a combination of transfer funding from the National Health Service, joint funding, a bigger share of increased resources from slow or moderate growth in the late 1980s, and some redistribution of resources as residential care of children is scaled down. The danger is that these groups – as in the National Health Service – will remain Cinderella services. A policy of positive discrimination is required, including the allocation of social work service. This policy would have implications for social work training, particularly for the mentally and the physically handicapped groups. Within this latter group special attention should be given to reviewing services for those with visual or hearing impairment, and generally improving the quality of service.

There is at present a much needed growth of specialist literature for the different client groups. For example, general books on the elderly (Brearley 1975; Rowlings 1981) are also complemented by specialist books on particular forms of care such as residential care for the elderly (Brearley 1977; Clough 1981). This trend should do much to clarify the application of more general social work principles and practice precepts to the needs of different groups.

Chapter six
MANPOWER, STRUCTURES AND TRAINING

DIFFERENTIAL USE OF MANPOWER

The concern expressed about the tasks and skills of social workers and whether they need re-thinking arises in a context where problems in the personal social service may be ascribed to inefficient use of manpower rather than other causes: i.e. lack of training opportunities or inappropriate training; defective management or organisational structures; conflicting expectations from the public, agencies and profession; overall shortage of trained manpower; lack of other resources. Periodic concern with the nature and level of skills required in social work and the shortage of manpower is not new. The Younghusband Carnegie Reports (1947 and 1951), the Younghusband Report (HMSO 1959), and the Birch Report (HMSO 1976), are among the more notable expressions of this concern. In the field of residential care the Williams Committee Report (1967) and the CCETSW Working Party Report (*Residential Work is a Part of Social Work* 1973) tried to clarify such issues. The underlying pressure has been powered by the expansion of personal social services since 1948 as a result of increased needs and awareness of social needs, and the general attempt to shift from philosophies of institutionally based service to community service. Much of the legislation of the last three decades (e.g. Mental Health Act 1959, a series of Children Acts, Chronically Sick and Disabled Act 1970) represents the formal societal response to these personal needs and philosophy. As a prelude to discussing some of the issues, a brief statement of the numbers of fieldwork staff is necessary. Table 7 shows the number of fieldwork staff (whole-time equivalents) for England and Wales in 1979:

The total number of senior social workers, social workers, trainees and social work assistants had increased from 14,633 in 1973 to

Table 7. Number of social work staff, 1979, England and Wales (whole-time equivalents)

	England	Wales	Total	%
Management and supervisory staff	3,250.1	249	3,499.1	12.7
Senior social workers	4,932.3	214	5,146.3	18.7
Social workers	12,930.7	784	13,714.7	50.0
Trainees	1,048			
Social work (welfare) assistants	3,288.1	204	5,074.6	18.5
Community workers	534.5			
	25,983.7	1,451	27,434.7	99.9
Total local authority personal social services staff			193,613.8	
Social workers and senior social workers as % of all fieldwork staff			68.8	(w.t.e.)
All social work staff as % of total personal social services staff			14.2	(w.t.e.)

Source: *Health and Personal Social Service Statistics, England and Wales*

20,499 in 1974, 22,095 in 1977 and just under 24,000 in 1979.

Social workers in social services departments form only about one-seventh of all personal social services staff and increased by around 50 per cent in the period 1973–77. This expansion has to be weighted against the increased range of responsibility, increase in need and large and more complex range of provision within departments which have already been described. After the establishment of all the social services departments in 1971 and the Central Council for Education and Training in Social Work, training also expanded with an enlarged proportion of newly trained or unqualified workers. The general philosophy of social work courses shifted from preparing social workers for work with particular client groups (children, the mentally ill, etc.) to preparing them for work with a variety of clients and problems – a general purpose social worker. Not surprisingly, psychiatrists were especially critical of what they viewed as a deterioration in quality of 'earmarked' social work service in the mental health field. Since the mid-1970s there has been a growing trend towards some degree of specialisation by client group in fieldwork services; residential services have remained structured on client group lines.

Social work 2000

This, in a crudely abbreviated form, is the present position. Are there any general principles which can be applied to argue for any radical re-structuring of the tasks of social workers? Two sets of principles are important. One deals with the categorisation of tasks, and the other with the criteria for evaluating different patterns of staff deployment. Tasks can be categorised along several dimensions:

(a) complexity: simple, moderately complicated, complex;
(b) reference or target groups: children and families; mentally ill; elderly or elderly physically handicapped or chronically sick; young physically handicapped; mentally handicapped;
(c) type of activity: administration; direct care; activity to change attitudes/behaviour/social environment (this would include the range of social work methods);
(d) organisational context/location for the task performance: area office; school; hospital; health centre; day centre; residential establishment.

Discussion until now has centred on (a) and (b). It has been argued (Ch. 4) that a number of simple tasks can be identified, e.g. straightforward counselling, visiting the elderly, escort duties, transport of goods and aids, help with clubs and activities, contacting other welfare agencies. All these are tasks frequently performed by assistant (welfare) social workers. Additionally there seems to be an assumption that work with the elderly and the mentally and the physically handicapped is intrinsically less complex than work with children and families. These are groups which have in the past received the worst quality of resources from health and personal social services, and the assumption seems to be based on convention rather than evidence. In residential care the assumption that the work is less complex is a reason for the slow pace of change; direct care is categorised as a simple activity. Thus at present the categorisation of tasks along the four divisions has been largely arbitrary and conventional. There is a *prima facie* argument for assuming that simpler tasks can be picked out in the whole range of activities of social workers, not just in the selective way at present. Usually these tasks form a part of an overall plan of help and it cannot be assumed that all simple tasks should be performed by workers with less or different training. Analyses of service received by clients reveals a wide variety of services, often provided in combination with each other. For a whole group of tasks designed as simple to be provided exclusively by assistant social workers or volunteers is likely to lead to worse service for some clients as well as better service for others. Following a personal service rather than an industrial model implies a good deal of flexibility in the deployment of staff and decisions in relation to each individual case.

This brings us to the second set of principles which provides criteria for evaluating different models of staff categorisation and deployment. Staff deployment patterns should meet four criteria, although each criterion could be given a different weighting. Thus:
(a) feasibility/practicality;
(b) improved service to clients;
(c) maximising effective deployment of the most highly trained workers;
(d) cost effectiveness.

The 'feasibility' criterion means that constraint factors like cost, existing statutory requirements, acceptability to agencies, professional bodies and other welfare services, must be recognised. The improved service criterion is included to keep in mind that we cannot assume that a change which seems desirable by the other criteria will actually improve service. Maximising the effectiveness of the most highly trained workers is a criterion which would seem to underlie a good deal of the concern with social work performance. It could be misleading to assume that highly trained workers should never undertake what are seen as simple tasks. Solicitors, doctors and teachers all do straightforward jobs which could be done or are done by people with lower levels of training or no training at all, e.g. conveyancing for house-purchase, clarification and/or explanation of a straightforward medical, social or educational problem, weighing babies, listening to children read, correcting simple sums, etc. Whilst it is likely that the most highly trained workers will deal with the most complex problems, and develop innovatory and specialist services, it can be argued that it is most undesirable for them to deal exclusively with these. Many of the professional restrictions on lower-level workers performing tasks designed as complex are more the result of monopolistic self-interest than concern for clients. Social workers deal with a wide range of problems involving many different types of service, where the personal element in service is very important. This would imply that it is perfectly reasonable for them to cross the skill boundary and undertake simpler tasks in many situations. The converse is also true – those with less training should also at times be able to undertake types of service normally associated with higher-level training or a different type of training (e.g. CSS). Only in this way can a more productive flexibility be achieved which also promotes the process of skill diffusion or skill-drift. As newer, more difficult, methods of working are developed, there should be a constant process of diffusion horizontally and vertically. Methods seen as difficult when first used become stand/normal/routine in the next generation. If highly trained professionals slow down this process by rigid professional demarcation potential benefits to clients are lost. The last criterion, cost effectiveness, demands that a new model of staff deployment must yield substantial savings/improvements in service if it involves major re-arrangement of existing patterns. For example, more rigid task classification according to types of worker may immediately imply greater numbers of staff (particularly at the lower level) which is an additional cost.

Social work, with its varied but distinctive array of functions and activities, resembles Crewe station, an exceedingly drab and uninviting but vital communications centre for the welfare state and society. It is also like a stock exchange trading not in stocks and shares but in the moral and social brokerage of a pluralist society. The present discussion suggests that the search for a rigid set of tasks rationally sub-divided and allocated according to the status and training of grades of workers is bound to fail if pursued beyond a certain point. As yet there is little evidence to demonstrate the superiority of different models. Some limited conclusions can be drawn which tentatively point to directions for change which will be consistent with responding to the challenges of the next two decades.

1. A range of simple tasks (broader than at present) can be delineated which can be carried out by workers with less or more limited training than CQSW; volunteers could, with appropriate back-up, also carry out these tasks. Care needs to be taken that this type of work is not carried out in a routine, impersonal manner divorced from the whole situations of families and groups. Such work may cover a range of clients and problems or be specific to client groups. The broader issue of specialisation is dealt with in the section on structures.
2. Such a designation between levels of complexity and the use of different levels/types of work should not preclude qualified social workers from undertaking simple tasks, if they form part of a larger plan of service and the client receives a more continuous and consistent service as a result. This is always a matter of judgement.
3. Fully qualified workers should make a key contribution in dealing with the more complex work, using methods requiring greater skill and knowledge, and developing new methods.

4. The partnership of different levels of workers and differentiation of tasks requires effective supervision, direction and support, and tends to imply that team models are likely to provide the kind of flexibility argued for here.
5. The evaluation of cost, the benefits to client, and feasibility is vital to ensure that new models which may be expensive in themselves and could involve organisational upheaval, are not introduced as a new fad which then becomes embedded in the system.

Social work is fortunate in not yet having committed itself to the rigidly stratified professional models of law, medicine and teaching. It still has the option of a more open-ended and dynamic approach to providing service with mixed levels and types of worker without fossilised demarcations which have little to do with improving the quality of service to clients.

INSTITUTIONS AND STRUCTURES

The regular use of a wider range of methods, using different types of worker in flexible combinations and developing more systematic though tension-laden relationships with other welfare services are all directions for the future which will affect residential- and day-care services as well as fieldwork services. It is clear that these developments have taken firmer shape in the 1970s and will gain a new impetus in the 1980s and 1990s. This view emphasises continuity as well as change but would maintain the impossibility of putting the clock back. The changes of the 1970s have, in fact, given social work a more secure foundation on which to build. For this reason clarity is needed about the sense of crisis and foreboding expressed in the last five to ten years. The sources are numerous and need stating before focusing on the future structures which should provide the context for social work practice.

Large-scale disquiet about the deaths of children at risk in their own homes began with Maria Colwell. In this and a number of deaths, the judgement of social workers was questioned, revealing contradictory expectations that children should and should not be removed from the community. Yet as important as these shades of opinion in many of the child tragedies was the story of administrative ineptitude or poor communication within and between services. There is still a stronger feeling with social workers than with doctors that if a child is seriously injured by an adult, or if a mentally ill person commits suicide, or if an elderly person dies of neglect in their own home that somehow the social worker and 'the welfare' are responsible. There is an unwillingness to accept that if large numbers of individuals experience deprived environments and severe emotional stress a proportion of them are going to behave or be affected in ways which anger or upset the general community. On the whole social workers, unlike doctors, cannot bury their mistakes so easily.

After 1971 psychiatrists were often critical of the frequently reduced quantity and standard of service they received from social workers in social services departments, in contrast to the more predictable service from mental welfare officers. After 1974 this feeling was exacerbated when management of psychiatric social work staff in hospitals was transferred to social services departments. Expansion of the latter and local government re-organisation broke the continuity which many psychiatrists had previously experienced. They were also coming into contact with more unqualified or inexperienced workers, or workers with less specialised training in mental health. It could be argued that psychiatrists and others were quite right to want some degree of specialised social work service, but wrong to criticise the concept of a general social worker as a part of the social services; psychiatrists would not argue for the destruction of the general practitioner services because there is a need for psychiatrists. It is worth noting that far from dismissing social work, many psychiatrists were pleading for more and better social work staff.

A deep unease has also permeated social work because of alleged ineffective and inappropriate methods. The sociological critique of casework/counselling in the 1960s was carried forward to the 1970s and supported by a number of studies revealing on average little change in clients as a result of social work intervention. This internal crisis of confidence was also fed by the many studies of ineffective residential care. Some of the criticism was well-founded and the late 1970s have seen a much greater emphasis on establishing clear objectives and tasks over a limited period combined with a greater use of social learning models to underpin intervention. Part of the criticism was misplaced. This was because most of the studies were of clients with substantial personal and environmental problems; it was unrealistic to assume that either counselling or very limited modification of the environment would have a magical cure effect. Also, evaluation was largely confined to social work methods which had the aim of behaviour/attitude change. Earlier discussion has argued that other areas of social work activity –

assessment, linking with other agencies and resources, straightforward advice, information and counselling – involving clients without major problems are equally important. If we judged medicine solely on its success with severe cancers we would rightly be accused of unfairness.

Some of these professional and public anxieties coalesce in pinpointing the structure of the social services departments as bureaucratic and top-heavy, but clearly have other origins. Nevertheless there are some issues, particularly those of specialisation and coordination which link these anxieties and the structures of departments. The main issues identified here are, relationship of the social services department to the community; centralisation/decentralisation of services; area and team structures; specialisation. A brief comment is necessary about the alleged top-heavy management, of too many chiefs and not enough indians. Senior directing, managing, professional and advisory staff are 12 per cent of all social work staff; however, these functions spread across the whole staff and range of functions, not only social work staff. As a proportion of all personal social services staff this group forms under 2 per cent of the total. It would include directors of social service, assistant directors, principal assistants, training staff, area officers and their deputies, and research staff. There is plenty of room for discussing management functions and qualitative issues, but in terms of number of staff the top-heavy image of social services staff is largely a myth. Administrative and clerical staff, a separate category, form 10 per cent of local authority personal social services staff against almost 13 per cent in the health service. The picture of a rampant bureaucracy is misleading and displaces attention from the form of organisation to an easy target.

RELATIONSHIP WITH THE COMMUNITY

There is still widespread ignorance in the community about the detailed functions of social services departments and social workers. When the departments were formed, expectations that they would deal with all problems in the community were raised. Faced with potentially limitless demands on their services, departments drew in their horns and adopted a more defensive lower profile in the second half of the decade. As a local authority service there exists too a tradition of closed administrative, hard for citizens to penetrate. There is urgent need for a more general awareness of the full range of services which departments provide, and of types of provision which are in short supply. This can be achieved in a variety of ways – annual reports, a national booklet similar to that for social security benefits, local booklets and information leaflets about services for the elderly, handicapped, etc., use of the local press, good quality information and advice services. Measures like these would produce a more informed and understanding climate of social work and social services, and more appropriate and easier use of service by consumers.

In sensing needs and mobilising community resources, departments also require a presence at the local neighbourhood level. There are implications for the location of area offices, sub-offices, use of residential/day-care bases, and for the deployment of specialist community workers. Some would suggest that 'patchwork' case allocation and responsibility would achieve this aim. There are a variety of means but the aim of embedding services more securely in the local community system is clear enough. It is salutary that the section on Community in the Seebohm Report is still the most neglected.

Participation is another dimension of community involvement with departments. By participation is meant voting and influencing elected members, elected members' involvement with professionals in clarifying information and value of political issues and priorities; informing the general public and particular user groups of the structure and process of provision; creation of structures (co-option to professional working parties; formal consultation with user/community groups; evaluation of service by user groups); involvement of voluntary/community individuals and groups in the provision of service. At present this is predominantly in the form of elected and co-opted members of committees, and in supporting voluntary services and volunteers. Extension of participation in identifying need and formulating service should be a major objective at the local level to attempt to structure services in a unique configuration for that locality.

Complaints by users can create conflict and general dissatisfaction. Most departments have no form of quasi-independent procedure for citizens to have complaints adjudged if they feel they have been refused service without good reason or the service provided has been deficient. Availability of established complaints procedures with at least some degree of independence would contribute to a more open and less defensive posture by departments. Clients must have some recourse to a fair procedure against seriously defective decisions or service provision.

Manpower, structures and training

CENTRALISATION/DECENTRALISATION

The implication of the discussion on relationships with the community is for greater decentralisation in the management of services. In the areas of budgeting, deployment of staff resources, identifying and responding to need there are cogent arguments for giving greater accountability and responsibility to area offices, and also for siting the staff in local offices. An area office covering an area with, say, 50,000–100,000 inhabitants may still be distant from any local communities. Bases in areas of high social need would seem to have economic advantages (less travelling, lower accommodation costs) and benefits to clients such as accessibility and greater responsiveness to local needs and resources.

Residential care can be managed in a decentralised manner – apart from specialised establishments serving the whole area – enabling links with the family and locality to be maintained, and rehabilitation to be arranged with minimum disruption to patterns of daily living. One of the potential benefits of greater decentralisation is the improved coordination between residential day-care and field services. The central budgeting process would be built upon area budgeting rather than the reverse. In a similar vein more administrative and clerical staff would be located at the area level as the central office divested itself of many executive tasks. Central management staff would be freer to concentrate on policy development, managing the total resource allocation to the department, payroll functions, planning and negotiating with other welfare agencies at a policy level, research and training, general procedural guidelines and monitoring.

AREA AND TEAM STRUCTURES

The service which clients receive depends greatly upon their immediate contact with social workers. Their key roles in assessment, linking people with services and providing service themselves have already been discussed. A greater decentralisation from the centre to area also implies that at the next level there will be greater freedom for teams to manage and direct their own work. Various models operate at present.
1. Teams of general purpose social workers taking referrals and work from a given area, working independently of each other apart from consultation over case allocation. This pattern would also be consistent with 'patch' working where each worker or pair of workers is responsible for all work in a sub-area.

2. Teams containing specialists and generalists, but handling all the work in a given area. The specialists may handle work with particular client groups or complex problems, the boundaries being decided by regular team-meetings. Specialist groups and community workers as well as social work assistants may be a part of these teams:
3. A combination of intake team(s) covering all intake and short-term work, and long-term teams dealing with chronic problems or clients in long-term contact with personal social services. Specialists may be attached to long-term teams or be grouped to serve several teams.
4. Multi-function teams with each team member carrying a combination of generalised and specialist functions:
5. Specialist teams according to client groups, e.g. for children and families, the elderly and the physically handicapped, the mentally ill and mentally handicapped.
6. Multi-disciplinary teams including members of other helping professions.

There is insufficient evidence to show which of these models is superior to others. At the area level one of the key decisions is to adopt the model(s) which seem to fit the type of area and the balance of problems and service needed. It is inappropriate for a model to be determined from the centre for the whole of the department. A team in a small deprived inner-city area might be organised using models (2) to (3), whereas a dispersed area might be more suited to (1) or (5). Perhaps more important than the particular model is the method of teams collaboration. In developing group- and community-oriented service collaboration is needed to identify the most useful problems to be coped with by these methods and in establishing the service. The whole team has a development role. Care is needed that the team does not become exclusive and detract from formation of constructive links in the wider welfare network. In day-to-day work, whichever model is adopted, flexibility is required to cope with sickness, holidays and staff turnover. Another vital point of team functioning is the support of colleagues and resources of skill and time which other members have. The role of the team leader has as much to do with maximising the potential of the team and its individual members as with supervising individual workers or taking decisions. The team leader and area officer posts are critical to the day-to-day functioning of the service and its development. Major problems arise where lack of delegation or lack of a democratic style of management place psychological and social constraints on imaginative collaboration between team members. In industry the middle-manager and foreman are recognised as people subject to conflicting demands from senior management and workers. This is equally so in personal social services and although the tensions of an intermediary position can never be entirely avoided, it is the job of senior management to set the tone and climate which ensure consistency of approach. In personal social services an authoritarian, rigidly controlling approach to management is out of place. Human services demand human management on a human scale. Decentralisation, flexibility, and team structures which foster cooperation are most likely to achieve these demands. Parsloe (1978, 1981), Stevenson (1981) and Payne (1979) discuss the issues of social service teams in greater detail and also deal with development of specialisation which is discussed briefly in the next section.

SPECIALISATION

Genericism and specialism have been part of the staple diet of social work debate for nearly three decades. Although as a straight-choice debating issue it is dead, it is very much alive, however if we ask what kind of specialists we want and how they should be used. For some of the reasons discussed at the start of this section departments are increasingly reverting to some form of specialist/practice organisation; some have gone so far as to adopt the model (5) pattern of team organisation. Nobody would now seriously dissent from the view that specialist workers are required for development, coordination and enhancement of good-quality practice with particular client groups, although this does not entail the team structures being built on specialist lines. Specialists in particular methods are another group of workers who may be located at central office, area or team level. Two general points have to be noted. Too great a degree of specialisation tends to give less emphasis to preventive and community orientation. To an extreme degree this is what we see in the health services with the greatest weight of resources going to acute care, not preventive health measures. Any concept of organising present social services around social hospitals should be anathema. The second point is that over-specialisation reduces flexibility of service and would deny general social workers of opportunities to increase their experience of and skills in dealing with particular client groups or problems. As yet there are no effective studies evaluating different types of specialist structuring and their relative benefits to clients. Therefore a pragmatic and experimental approach would be justified for several years yet. Guiding principles should be demonstrable improvements in service to clients and their communities and potential diffusion of skills and understanding to non-specialist workers. The lack of comparative evaluation of different structures would indicate that wholesale rebuilding of services along specialist lines would be counter-productive and uncertain in its effects on quality of service. All the problems encountered in the separate departments before re-organisation in 1971 would ultimately reappear, families and individuals with several different problems being dealt with by a confusing medley of workers. Stability of working relationships with other services can be as effectively maintained by stable area and team structures whether specialist or not. As with teaching, social work always has more staff turnover because of the high proportion of women workers (it was noticeable the earlier mental health departments had a preponderance of male workers), but after the rapid expansion of social work services 1965–75 a period of more general stability and continuity seems likely. Finally, it is worth considering an additional pattern of specialist working. For limited periods, where service to a client group or use of a method is recognised as deficient, formation of specialist task forces or project groups might be effective in stimulating change. A close liaison with training staff would be necessary to ensure diffusion of improved practice methods. Hey (1979) gives a valuable analysis of key assumptions on which specialisation is based, and stresses the links between specialisation, training and structures within social services departments.

EDUCATION AND TRAINING FOR SOCIAL WORK

The decade 1965–75 was remarkable for the changes in thought, practice and organisation of social work and personal social services. Merging of separate services within the social services departments and subsequent expansion, growing interest in group and community work, a parallel unification of separate training councils into the Central Council for Education and Training in Social Work, and legislative change (The Children and Young Persons Act 1969, The Chronically Sick and Disabled Persons Act 1970), all pointed to a more coherent pattern of service, extended responsibilities and a need for more trained staff to cope with the expansion and backlog of unqualified social workers. There was in training a considerable expansion which levelled off after 1975. The general concern with supplying the services with enough trained staff was reflected by the establishment of the Birch Committee in 1974, which reported in 1976. The British Association of Social Workers also published its policy statement *Social Work Education: The Way Ahead* in 1976. During this process, rumblings about the quality of courses and the questionable fit of their products with the requirements of social services departments have grown louder. Already the tendency to displace blame for some of the problems of social services departments and training courses has been noted. This issue is one of the several dimensions of education and training which need further discussion. The key areas are: the size and adequacy of the training system; the type and level of training; marking training and practice demands; establishing priorities for the future.

Before dealing with these issues a brief answer must be given to those who question whether training is needed at all, in spite of the indications so far of the range of knowledge, understanding and skills required of the social worker. The objections arise from the fact that in some studies of social work, untrained workers perform as well as, or only a little worse than, trained workers (Goldberg 1970), and also from the commonsense observation that trained and untrained workers often work alongside each other undertaking much the same work. One reply would be this: Since a vital part of learning any skill or competence is practice it is not surprising that many people, if placed in a work situation, will eventually acquire a good degree of skill; it would be expected that a wider range of variation in standards of practice would result. I suspect that if the professions of law, medicine and teaching permitted it, most people with a reasonable degree of intelligence and application could acquire most of the skills of doctors and lawyers in day-to-day practice by working alongside skilled practitioners. Thus the justification for recognised training schemes does not come from arguing that trained workers would always give better service than workers who acquire their skills by experience only. Education and training are justified by arguments of accountability, reliability of standards, and efficiency. Thus formal education and training shorten the period of learning, ensure that by and large basic standards of practice are met throughout the service and provide some degree of accountability for decent practice by the practitioner. In any service maintenance of a regular supply of reasonably skilled workers is probably best organised by an institutionalised form of training, although since learning practice skills is a central objective the training programme must afford systematic opportunities to practice under guidance and instruction. At the end of formal education and training programmes, it is illusory to expect that consolidation and continual learning is unnecessary. Many of the criticisms of newly trained social workers stem from failure to recognise this is as much from incompatibility between the course content and work content. In any case the course practice of social work students (usually one-third to one-half of the course) is carried out in social work agencies, who bear a major responsibility for the quality of practice experience. So the fact that often newly trained social workers are still 'green' or 'wet behind the ears' is no more remarkable than for newly trained doctors, teachers, nurses, and lawyers. Critics will complain that these arguments are complacent. It can only be replied that they apply to all forms of training, not just social work, and that acceptance of the arguments in no way assumes that particular forms of training are immutable or should not be subject to critical study. There will always be bad practice by a minority of trained practitioners. Without any form of reasonably coherent education and training system there is a much greater risk of poor and uneven service by practitioners.

The size and adequacy of the training system

The Central Council for Education and Training in Social Work, in its validating and promotional roles, has established changing priorities during the 1970s. The first priority was expansion of CQSW training, very successfully achieved in the period up to 1975–76. Very quickly the needs of residential staff were given priority, continuing the concern shown by the Home Office Central Training Council. After the report *Residential Work is a Part of Social Work* (CCETSW 1973), the policy adopted was bi-polar; encouragement of CQSW training for residential social workers (planning out the one-year residential social work courses) and development of a different type of training mainly for residential and day-care staff. Both these policies were implemented with the Certificate in Social Service Course starting in 1975. Increasing numbers of CQSW courses included residential social work options. The final component in a developing strategy to cover all social work and other personal social service staff was the push towards promoting post-qualifying training. From 1975 most parts of the country were gradually served by validated post-qualifying courses, which encouraged advanced practice, management, teaching and research skills.

By 1975-76 all the elements of an overall strategy for training were being implemented, but the ambitious range of target strategies set out by the Birch Report have had no chance of full implementation because of the increasingly bleak economic situation. Expansion of CQSW training for residential social workers and the Certificate in Social Work Service has been large in percentage terms since 1975, but falls well short of levels which would make a significant impact on services, given the relatively low proportion of trained staff in day and residential services. The levelling off in recruitment to all courses in the late 1970s has been affected by a combination of financial constraints. Social services departments, while protected to some degree from the real decline in local government expenditure since 1975, are financing fewer trainees and secondments, have been unable to support post-qualifying training to any substantial degree, and are at most only able to support CSS training at present levels. Financial retrenchment is also endangering in-service training and staff development to some degree. From the point of view of intending students, non-graduate students are finding it more difficult to obtain LEA grants which are not mandatory for social work, as well as securing traineeships or secondments from departments. Graduates have the security of the DHSS grants but the stabilising of departments, with reduced opportunities for first promotion, have affected recruitment and led to a reduced proportion of men entering training, which was a marked feature of the 1960s and early 1970s. There is limited DHSS grant support for students on post-qualifying courses but even now all the available places on post-qualifying courses are not taken up. Thus, with the exception of CQSW training for fieldwork social work staff, the picture emerges of training for residential and day-care workers which has completely failed to match the increases in numbers. The numbers of staff in the following categories, for instance, increased substantially in 1974-77 (see Table 8).

This overall picture, apart from the initial thrust in CQSW training, indicates a less than enthusiastic attitude by central government towards residential and day-care staff. Central government, whether Labour or Conservatives are in power, is fundamentally unconcerned about adequacy of training for these groups, and has shown far more willingness to fund expensive capital projects of uncertain value than to fund the training for staff who will work in them. In the immediate future (up to 1983-84) the financial resources devoted to training will not expand, and educational in-

Table 8

	w.t.e. (thousands)			
	1974	1977	1979	Increase 1974–79
Adult training centres care staff	3.3	3.9	4.6	1.3
Day centres (mentally ill, elderly and physically handicapped) care staff	1.4	2.0	2.4	1.0
Homes for elderly and elderly mentally infirm care staff	6.7	7.8	9.2	2.4
Homes for the younger physically handicapped care staff	0.1	0.2		
Homes and hostels for the mentally ill and mentally handicapped care staff	1.8	2.5	3.1	1.3
Community homes for children and young persons in care, care staff	11.7	14.5	15.4	3.7
				9.7

Source: *DHSS and Welsh Office Local Authority Social Service Statistics*

stitutions as well as social services departments will find it hard to maintain the present level of training.

TYPE AND LEVEL OF TRAINING – QUALIFYING COURSE

Different patterns of training have been reviewed in the last section and it is useful to summarise (see Table 9) the types and levels of training, the form of training, and the target groups.

In terms of course orientation CSS and post-qualifying courses are more specialist, whereas the CQSW is a generalist training. The reason for this is that entrants to CSS and post-qualifying courses are already in employment in the social services and have a clearer conception of what they want to concentrate on in their studies; much of the content and application of these courses can be chosen by the student so long as he conforms to the broad pattern and requirements. The posts being prepared for by the CSS usually have a restricted range of responsibility in terms of client group, work-

Table 9. Main forms of education and training validated by CCETSW

Recruitment group	Type/Level	Form	Posts prepared for
Graduates 20 years and over. Non-graduates under 25 years with O and A levels. Non-graduates over 25 years without formal qualifications.	CQSW (1 or 2 year) training and some 4 year courses.	1 or 2 years. Predominantly full-time. Approx. half period in practice placements.	Mainly field social workers. Also residential social workers, community workers, etc.
O and A level holders. Older students without formal qualifications.	Certificate in Social Service.	2–5 years. Day release whilst in employment. Modular academic work, supervised practice.	Residential care and day-care staff. Assistant social workers or social service officers.
CQSW holders with at least 2 years post-qualifying experience.	Post-qualifying.	Part-time or full-time. Minimum 60 days, up to 1 year.	Advanced practice; advisers; senior social workers; managers social work teams; training officers; researchers.

setting and tasks. At the post-qualifying level students have mostly selected a client group, practice-method, research, or teaching management skills as the focus of interest. With the CQSW most entrants are new to social work and are preparing to work in a very broad field; they may have no clear idea of areas of specialist interest or work, or their ideas may change as they gain experience in training. The range of methods they will employ is wide as is the range of problems and the client groups they are likely to meet. Most CQSW courses now incorporate optional choices in certain areas of academic study and allow a degree of specialisation in choice of placements. However, the functions and methods discussed earlier demand both a strength of understanding in social sciences which inform social work, and also extensive knowledge of social service systems and a variety of skills. If this rationale is accepted it is inevitable that some knowledge and experience of particular client groups and methods cannot be as extensive as when workers were trained as mental welfare officers or child care officers. A generalist training is by definition unable to give extensive in-depth attention to all client group and practice areas. The crucial role of assessment in the community, working with individuals, families and groups, and liaising with other services cannot be undertaken satisfactorily without a broad training. No doubt some degree of specialist study can be introduced into general courses, and modifications can make generalist courses more effective, but the need for a group of workers with a firm grasp of environmental and psychological pressures in modern life, the problems they give rise to, and ways of trying to resolve or cope with them, cannot be overstated. One of the reasons for resisting the ever more detailed categorisations of tasks and their allocation to specialists is that in personal social service we are dealing with people and not things. Division of labour and patterns of organisation found in industry and commerce are not necessarily valid in human service organisations. To a certain degree the overlapping boundaries between different types of tasks and worker are essential. A further argument for a generalist training is that the approach to specialised roles and tasks will be different. Even within the CSS and post-qualifying studies students with a mainly specialised focus need some more general framework; in the CSS, for example, this is provided in the common Unit at Study.

I have argued that the generalist orientation of social work courses (incorporating limited degrees of specialist experience and study through options) since the early 1970s is valid by virtue of the range of work which social workers undertake and the flexibility in deployment which a general training gives. Departments have found this situation difficult to adapt to, and the relationship of training to agency practice and requirements is the next theme.

Matching training and practice demands

It is an illusion to think that there can ever be an exact congruence between the context of education and training and the requirements of agencies. Educational institutions will be attempting to distill the most up-to-date knowledge and practice patterns to communicate to students. These advances are patchily present in departments, representing innovatory thinking and experience in a minority of agencies. There is also a generation gap. Many senior staff will have trained under a different pattern which is more likely to have been specialist with an emphasis on casework; they will not always welcome different approaches and tend to be critical of less detailed knowledge and lack of experience in newly trained workers. Such factors were strong features of the position in the early and mid-1970s, with a larger proportion of newly trained workers in departments. Most criticism of training from the departments can be explained by such factors and resistance of the implication that departments would have eventually to provide additional systematic experience during the first year of employment. Even in 1959 the Younghusband Report had suggested the need for a 3-year training was desirable, but accepted that central government would be unwilling to finance such an extension. Even more so now, if the principle of a generalist training is accepted, there are two alternatives if breadth and depth of experience are to be gained following CQSW training. The first alternative would be a third year in training as part of the CQSW course mainly spent in supervised practice covering all client groups in turn, consolidating basic skills and extending the range of methods. Regular seminar/recall periods would complement fieldwork teaching. In this alternative the practitioner remains a student attached to the course. The second alternative is for the student to enter employment for a probationary/accreditation period. Again there would be formal supervision and structured learning opportunities, but evaluation and assessment would be primarily a matter for CCETSW (or possibly a Social Work Council) and the agency staff, but with some educational involvement.

Both alternatives would require additional resources. The second would continue the trend towards closer cooperation between courses and agencies, but unless there were an agreed practice curriculum this could lead to accreditation or fulfilment of a probationary period with highly variable standards. Financial limits will delay action for a few years but there is all the more reason to use the available time for consultation and to work out specific schemes in more detail. The revised guidelines for CQSW courses, at present undergoing a final drafting before implementation, lay more stress on the practice component and delineate the academic curriculum in rather more detail than hitherto. However they cannot ensure the breadth and depth of experience, which present CQSW courses, with the remit to train general purpose social workers, are unable to provide.

Other models, reverting to apprentice-types of training, would emulate medical training with either one or two years in social science training, followed by two years of departmental training, with course tutors and agency training staff closely involved in teaching and practice. Students in training would follow a closely regulated practice curriculum, covering the range of client groups, problems and social work methods.

Any of these possibilities could achieve the desired result. All would cost money except, perhaps, the last – if a purely academic curriculum were followed for a year, releasing course staff resources to work educationally in agencies. No one should be in any doubt, nevertheless, that whatever improvements are made in present social work courses, e.g. more experiential teaching, simulation, they will not solve the fundamental problem of providing sufficient teaching and experience across all the areas of work with which a social worker deals.

Educational and training priorities for the future

Out of the present discussion several clear priorities can be discerned. Some will have to wait for implementation, but even these can be worked on in the meantime. Implementation depends on changed attitudes and the ability to convince politicians and the public that financial outlay is worthwhile and leads to better services for clients.

1. Expansion of CSS and post-qualifying studies when resources permit.
2. Implementing accreditation/probationary year in CQSW training, alternatively adopting a purely academic social science/social work curriculum for either one or two years with a systematic practice curriculum. The accreditation/probationary year model could, unless carefully regulated, result in considerable additional expenditure with uncertain results.
3. Reform of the funding system for training.
4. Positive discrimination to ensure adequate access of residential and day-care staff to CSS, and CQSW and post-qualifying courses.
5. Clear cooperation between course and agency staff in developing models, and to prepare innovatory teaching patterns for (2) above. The present sharp divisions between agencies and educational institutions are already softening, and further interlocking and cooperation is vital. This collaboration is also essential in the development of in-service training.
6. Little has been said about course content in this section. Earlier

discussions would imply greater importance being assigned to administrative skills, and to teaching on residential, group and community practice within integrated methods schema. Similarly, greater weight should be given to teaching and experience with the elderly, children, physically handicapped and mentally handicapped persons, mentally ill persons, the unemployed and ethnic minorities.

Chapter seven
CONCLUDING DISCUSSION

In trying to picture social work over the next two decades a way of approaching it has been attempted which is neither crudely deterministic nor so utopian that it loses touch with reality. How it will turn out depends on many imponderables but also on many factors which may be anticipated. It also depends on how the various individuals and groups within social work react to the larger context and the kind of values and goals they seek to work for. The value which society places on social work and the personal social services will depend partly on the quality of the social work response and its ability to communicate effectively with very different audiences, i.e. the general public, other welfare institutions, users of its services, and elected representatives at central and local government level. Social work will survive, but the question to ask is, 'In what form?' As a highly technical and professionalised part of social services offering very specialist service out of touch with the greater part of the needs of its clients? As a purely administrative institution testing eligibility and rationing service? As the iron hand of the state in a velvet glove, pacifying discontent and potential disorder? As a quasi-religious social movement aiming to convert society to values it holds dear? Some elements of all these potentialities will find a home in the future social work. There remains also the potential for an open-end adaptable social institution exercising a dual influence: responding, creatively and imaginatively to changing social needs, and feeding and influencing other social institutions and society at large with the understanding generated in that process. What are the constraints and possibilities which might shift social work in one direction or another?

POSSIBLE SCENARIOS

The world and OECD economic development prospects were ex-

Concluding discussion

amined earlier. We can postulate three basic types of scenario adapted from *Interfutures* (1979) for the British economy and outline, albeit crudely, the implications for the welfare state and social work in each of them.

Scenario 1: Maximum Growth

High economic growth accompanied by structural change:

Social consequences Increased unemployment in the next five to ten years, decreasing in the 1990s; social conflict over distribution of added wealth; greater inequality; disadvantaged growth outcasts; emphasis on individualism and self-reliance; greater regional inequalities; more violence, crime, mental illness, divorce.

Welfare State Part of growth wealth to maintain and expand services, or, more likely, pressure to reduce State Welfare and increase private/occupational/charity welfare; uneven reductions within the State welfare sector, social security maintaining relatively high expenditure with substantial reductions in housing and education, with personal social services experiencing a lesser reduction; selectivity maintained or extended with increased charges for many State services; two tiers of relatively high standard private welfare and low standard public welfare.

Social work Static or slightly reduced in quantity; either limited role in the direction of basic relief functions, administering gradually deteriorating personal social services and/or concentration on 'expert' counselling services with growth of private practice social work. An alternative conflict response would be a political and social advocacy role, whilst administering static or declining personal social services. Re-emergence of fundamental conflict between conservative and radical traditions in social work (between personal and political ideologies discussed by Halmos).

Scenario 2(a): Slow to moderate growth with structural change

Social consequences Social problems increase as in scenario (1) but not to the same degree. A slower pace of change allows more orderly social accommodation and adaptation of social institutions. The possibility of a pluralist social consensus around the balance of economic and social goals is more viable. Problems may appear similar to scenarios (1) and 2(b) but are more likely to be resolved in the late 1960s and in the 1990s.

Welfare State   Maintained at static or very slowly increasing levels in real terms; slower growth of private/occupational welfare; pressure on social security expenditure in terms of unemployment and supplementary benefits not as great as in (1); better coordination of social policy of central and local government departments is possible and there is scope for reducing regional imbalance.

Social work   Maintained at present levels in real terms; a major role in contributing to an orderly shift from institutional to community care as part of personal social services strategy in collaboration with other social services (predominantly with health and housing and also with social security, education and police). A broad range of social work functions and service maintained, with new patterns of service and forms of cooperation with voluntary resources; greater community participation. Protection of social minorities and 'growth outcasts' is a major function in the first decade.

Scenario 2(b): Slow to moderate growth without structural change

Social consequences   This scenario may appear more positive in the short term, with fewer social problems generated by structural change. Unemployment remains, however, at relatively high levels and could worsen in the late 1980s and 1990s as the economy slows down and is ill-adapted to new technologies and new international patterns of trade. The trend is for this scenario to turn into scenario (3) in the 1990s.

Social work and the Welfare State   As 2(a), but just as the positive changes described become potentially accessible, there is pressure to reduce Welfare State expenditure as social problems begin to intensify. Features of the short-term scenario would be rigidity of response to needs partly associated with increased unionisation of Welfare State workers; in the late 1980s bitter conflict would show between sections of the welfare state as each tries to maintain its share of decreasing allocations to welfare; distributional problems become acute.

Concluding discussion

Scenario 3: No growth or decline

Social consequences Increased social conflict over distribution of declining national income; regional problems exacerbated; greater inequality; possible increases in crime, divorce and mental illness as in scenario (1) with even less chance of responding to them; increase in State authority and coercion as social disorder mounts; insularity and economic protectionism in relation to the rest of the world.

Welfare State Reduced real resources and increased problems; as services deteriorate flight into private/occupational welfare for a minority; fragmentation and conflict between different sectors of the Welfare State; social security maintains relatively high share of social services resources with education and housing and personal social services taking a disproportionate cut, and health services in an intermediate position.

Social work The relief functions are emphasised; rationing and social control functions dominate as resources decline and need increases; some lesser development of private practice as frustration with State standards grows; a strong minority advocacy function maintains a presence but is politically ineffective.

The description of these alternative scenarios is sketchy, incorporating only the main features. In our present period of economic difficulties it would be a mistake to assume that scenario 3 is already with us. It has to be recognised that in the last decade substantial growth has taken place in social security (child benefits, the new pension scheme, a range of benefits for the handicapped, chronically sick and disabled), health services, and a range of personal social services (home-helps, day-care, meals, aids and adaptations). Additional resources have not always led to demonstrable improvement in quality of service or benefits to users of the Welfare State, and it is facile to expect rapid rates of growth in the last decade to continue. Scenario 2(a) offers the most exciting possibilities for constructive social change accompanied by significant developments in the structure and coordination of services. Economically, it seems consistent with projections by the OECD, and the leeway which North Sea oil gives for alleviating the social consequences of structural change. The personal social service and social work scenario is consistent with the developments already discussed in greater detail. This demands a high degree of responsiveness, imagination and willingness to change structures and institutions in a climate very different from 1965–75. We have grown used to introducing change as services expand quickly; often this is by a process of accretion – simply adding the new while leaving the old relatively unchanged. Undertaking major shifts with only low to moderate growth, interrupted by some periods of no growth at all, requires a different mentality. Changing or expanding particular services will only be achieved by reducing another service or other changes in use of resources. This climate of change will meet with many vested interests and objections, and will place a heavy burden on managerial staff in working for change with other staff and the community. There may be areas of service where statutory services provide a basic and adequate service, where community resources provide additional quality elements. An example of this is in homes for the elderly; where furniture is often provided, should it not be the norm for residents to provide their own from their homes, and only where this is inadequate, for the State to provide. Various types of jointly funded provision, whether between statutory services or between them and voluntary services, may be far less wasteful than some present patterns – day nurseries, nursery schools, playgroups and child-minding form an uncoordinated spread of service unevenly through the community, although each shares many common aims with the others. Housing policies can encourage relations to look after their elderly, or enable an old person to live near relatives. Volunteers can enable social workers to spend more time with those with serious social problems or on preventive work. Joint programmes to prevent and cope with delinquency are much better than a set of uncoordinated services, which may overlap and be wasteful of resources.

SOCIAL WORK VALUES

Response to the possible scenarios depends on the balance of values within the social work profession. One set of values is incorporated in professional ethics, that of confidentiality and the prime duty of service to the client. A second relates to the dignity of individuals – acceptance, self-determination, non-judgemental attitudes. A third relates to the need for the social environment to provide conditions which promote welfare and personal and social fulfilment. This latter set, by no means exclusive to social work, is consistent with a broader cluster of values such as: reducing financial and social in-

Concluding discussion

equality; working for greater social justice; extending tolerance towards minority values in a pluralist society; fostering participation by citizens in social institutions. The individualism of the past was associated with the charitable origins of modern social work. The present and future form of individualism is more firmly tied in with socially oriented values which key into concepts of interdependency in society. Analysis along the lines of the present study argues that social work will only be of maximum service to society if full recognition is given to relationships with the personal social services, other welfare institutions, the economy, and the cultural development.

Social work is not a homogeneous institution. It is an abstract concept loosely referring to groups of social institutions – courses, agencies, professional organisations – and the varied individuals and groups working within them. It connotes the wide range of activities undertaken and the values which underpin them. In the main, the activities are ordinary and undramatic representing the institutionalised concern of society for those enmeshed in personal and social difficulty. Although there is no justification for assuming that their work is of greater moral worth or social usefulness than commercial, industrial or scientific work (or other forms of welfare activity), social workers are at an advantage in experiencing and analysing the effects of economic and social development on the lives of citizens. It is an element in their accountability to society that this experience and information is relayed to the rest of society for people to choose what to do about it. An equally important part of being accountable to society is evaluating the usefulness of the activities which social workers undertake. If the various forms of social work activity are to be more than ritual absolution of the society's conscience, evaluation and research into the whole range of functions is essential. Most research so far has focused on the functions relating to significant personality/behaviour change in people who have often experienced severe personal or social stress over long periods. It is hardly surprising that it is not at present very effective, but this is no reason for not continuing to find forms of help which are effective. In contrast, relatively little effort has gone into evaluating the remainder of the functions and methods of working with less intractable problems. Evaluation in these areas might reveal a different story. The main point is that social work and social workers should positively welcome research and evaluation if politicians and the general public are to be reasonably assured that public money for social work is well spent. Accountability has another dimension in relation to the people served by social work. They need to be assured that social workers are competent and that they have some say in the way problems are defined and choices made about service. Thus professional openness, acceptance of regulation and discipline (e.g. from a Social Work Council) and wider participation are essential if relations between clients, the public and social workers are not to be blighted by excessive professional distance, secrecy and defensiveness.

For individual social workers the weightings given to the values vary considerably. They have trained at different times when the emphasis on particular methods and dimensions of social action and concern has oscillated. Social workers in medical settings have tended not unnaturally to model their concepts of professional ethics on that of medicine, whereas community and other social workers may emphasise the socially oriented part of their ethics rather more. Even so it could be said that social workers' political and social beliefs would nowadays tend to be left of centre in matters of social policy but still with a pretty wider scatter amongst individuals. This could hardly be different. The major advances in social science since the nineteenth century have all supported environmentalist and social structure explanations for social and personal problems rather than solely individualistic explanations. Social workers also have the evidence of their own eyes in which somewhere approaching a third of the population receives incomes of supplementary benefit level or slightly above this level; a high proportion of social work clients are from this third of the nation. In social policy, therefore, social workers generally support more equalising and universally based provision with attention to the very unequal wealth and income distribution in society. Professional associations like BASW have a strong record in supporting social policy proposals which, if implemented, would diminish the need for social workers. At the level of working with particular individuals, groups and communities social workers with vastly different philosophies – ranging from fairly traditional catholic to solid Marxist – often work in a very similar way. In part this is because it is people and their situations which tend to determine the appropriate response to problems. Also, within social work training the combination of sociology and psychology on the whole gives weight to both individual and social factors, not just the one or the other. Thus social workers, some of whom may have entered social work with powerful beliefs, religious, humanist or political, become pragmatically oriented when face to face with clients. They attempt

Concluding discussion

to analyse the social situations confronting them with a broad and flexible array of understanding from the social sciences and an appreciation of the moral dilemmas in social intervention. It is quickly borne in on them that schemes of broad reform – housing, income maintenance, education – do not inevitably change people's personalities or magically make them better people; neither does personal intervention in the manner of social work. Better, more equally distributed, resources are justified by wider concepts of social justice and longer-term goals, but it is in the areas of articulation of services to individual need, small-scale social and personal change, and protection against specific disadvantage and handicap where social work is at present most effective.

In facing the next two decades social work values will not be immutable but in shifting constellations, reflecting societal cultural change and how the constituent groups in social work resolve internal emphases and tensions. The worst outcome would be a retreat into conservative social technocracy within a professional model which places highest value on expert techniques, professional mystique and social distance from those in need. Equally damaging would be a spurious progression on the basis of a single ideology such as Marxism. Our challenge is to fashion the kind of limited consensus, containing a healthy conflict, but based on meeting the needs of dependent and disadvantaged groups in a spirit of partnership. The challenge will be met more effectively if it is based on the broad range of functions which social workers carry out and responds keenly to the possible developments and scenarios which have been discussed. Social workers will need to make their voices heard. Others will listen if the voice is not too shrill or sanctimonious but speaks with a degree of humility and recognition of our limits, as we try to understand and contribute to the resolution of human problems and society.

There is a cautionary note which must be entered here if social workers and their values are not to run counter to fundamental concepts of democracy and freedom. The paternalistic syndrome can be seen at work just as much in 'social engineering' socialist approaches or in right-wing intolerance of minorities. Self-determination (McDermott 1978), one of the central ethical values for social workers means that only in the direct situation involving serious danger to a person or others is intervention justified against the wishes of the person. Earlier discussion of participation and choice is related to this general principle. Because the choice of individuals to use a service or not, or to choose what kind of service, is also dependent on the types of provision available, a say in policy as well as the rights to refuse service or to select the form of service is vital. It also implies a range of provision within which people can make choices. Voucher schemes, as suggested by the IEA are one way of achieving this although, as frequently pointed out, if voucher values are pitched at too low a level the present distribution of incomes would ensure that for the poorest section of the community choice could be more restricted than at present with a two-tier private and State sector developing. In the end, greater choice and freedom depend upon differentiated programmes of services being available and the attitudes of professionals in the services to users of the services.

Much of the analysis in earlier chapters has outlined future prospects for personal social services and social work and the parameters of external conditions and constraints which influence those prospects. Some objectives have been set out with greater or lesser degrees of definition. How we get 'from here to there', to use Rowtow's phrase, depends greatly on the degree of administrative responsiveness within the services and their staffs. In looking at the functions of social workers more emphasis has been placed on administrative competence than is usual in many social work texts. Many people view administration as a necessary evil getting in the way of service provision. The view here is that skilled and flexible administration is one of the central hallmarks of the good social worker. But it is administration informed by and grounded in a firm base of moral principles, rather than a mechanical conception of departmental requirements. Alan Keith-Lucas, apart from Barbara Wootton (Wootton 1959), is the most consistent exponent of this view. Keith-Lucas writes (1957):

Administrative responsiveness is, in fact, a highly complex subject. Probably in my group of decisions there both is and ought to be some responsiveness to all of the values ... 'the will of the people', 'the truths of science', and the 'moral order', as well as perhaps 'the needs of the personality'.

Nevertheless, the solutions that can be proposed tend to suggest that the most important criterion will be found in the moral sphere.

Keith-Lucas argues that too great a reaction to public opinion will inevitably distort service provision (this could certainly be argued with respect to non-accidental injury to children, and community attitudes to the mentally ill). Similarly, too great a reliance on social science knowledge and research into social work and personal social services, without recognising its limitations, will distort

Concluding discussion

decisions in individual cases and in policy. Ultimately, these adjuncts to deciding if and how to meet personal and social need have to be imbued with a sense of moral principles of which self-determination is a key constituent. The social worker is not only a relationships technician, but is or ought to be an educated and humane public servant, as sensitive in the art of administration as in casework or groupwork. What binds these functions of service-giving therapy and administration together is the thread of common moral principles. Adherence to this moral foundation is our main hope for 'getting from here to there' in open-ended ways which do not inviolate the dignity and freedom of individuals and groups. The outcome, whether similar or different from the present analysis, will be validated or invalidated by the integrity of the social processes we choose to reach them.

Appendix A
TRENDS IN SELECTED SOCIAL SERVICES IN ENGLAND AND WALES (THOUSANDS)

	1972			1975		
	Eng.	Wales	Total	Eng.	Wales	Total
1. Persons supported by local authorities in homes for the elderly and younger physically handicapped	113.5	6.9	120.4	120	7.9	127.9
2. Places in local authority training centres for mentally handicapped	27.2	1.6	28.8	34.2	2.1	36.3
3. Places in local authority homes and hostels for the mentally ill (staffed and unstaffed)	2.0	0.2	2.2	2.5	0.3	2.8
4. Places in local authority homes and hostels for the mentally handicapped (staffed and unstaffed)	5.3	0.2	5.5	7.5	0.3	7.8
5. Home-help cases (1 April – 31 March)	473.9	28.3	502.2	615.0	33.5	648.5
6. Meals served in centres (1 April – 31 March)	888.8	370	9,258	14,418	557	14,975
7. Meals on wheels served (1 April – 31 March)	15,833	896	16,829	23,482	1,506	24,988
8. Children in local authority care	86.5	4.1	90.6	94.2	4.9	99.1
9. Places in day nurseries and nursery groups maintained by local authorities or by voluntary bodies under agency agreements	25.0	–	25.0	28.7	0.3	29.0

Source: DHSS *Health and Personal Social Services Statistics: Welsh Office.*

Appendix A

		1977			1978			1979	Percentage increase
Eng.	Wales	Total	Eng.	Wales	Total	Eng.	Wales	Total	1972–77
126.9	8.0	134.9	128.1	8.1	136.2	127.1	8.3	135.4	12
38.7	2.4	41.1	40.8	2.4	43.2	42.1	2.4	44.5	40
3.1	0.2	3.3	3.3	0.3	3.6	3.6	0.3	3.9	51
9.8	0.3	10.1	10.7	0.5	11.2	11.4	0.5	11.9	89
665.1	38.6	703.7	692.5	40.2	732.7	730.3	42.3	772.6	40
16,565	638	17,203	15,300	597	16,397	14,800	532	15,332	86
24,607	1,753	25,360	25,300	1,774	27,074	26,200	1,840	28,040	51
96.2	4.9	101.1	94.2	4.9	99.1	95.1	4.9	100.0	11.5
24.9	0.4	25.3	27.7	0.4	28.1	28.3	0.4	28.7	0.1

Appendix B
SOCIAL SERVICES DEPARTMENT STAFF IN ENGLAND AND WALES (MAIN CATEGORIES). (WHOLE-TIME EQUIVALENT)

	1974				
	Eng.	Wales	Total	Eng.	Wales
1. Social worker (headquarters and area office)	21,680	1,068	22,748	24,300	133,815
2. Other headquarters and area office staff	16,139	722.4	16,861.4	50,400	886
3. Adult training centres	5,118	341.8	5,459.8	59,000	418
4. Day centres for the mentally ill, elderly and physically handicapped	2,940	94.1	3,934.1	4,400	210.3
5. Day nurseries and part-time nursery groups	8,156	27.5	8,183.5	8,600	44.7
6. Home-help staff	42,388	2,798.5	45,186.5	44,900	2,956.8
7. Residential accommodation for the elderly physically handicapped and elderly mentally infirm	45,169	3,044.7	48,213.7	50,400	3,222.9
8. Homes for the mentally disabled	3,544	150.4	188,500	5,500	304.8
9. Community homes for children and young persons in care	19,123	997.1		22,200	1,219.5
Total social service department staff	166,197	9,496.7	175,693.7	188,500	10,700.2

Source: DHSS *Health and Personal Social Services Statistics*: Welsh Office Economic Services Division.
Total staff Personal Social Services, England and Wales, 1000s (w.t.e.)

1971	1972	1973	1974	1975	1976	1977	1978	1979
113.4	143.0	159.6	175.7	180.5	194.5	198.6	203.2	204.7

Appendix B

1977	1978					1979
Total	Eng.	Wales	Total	Eng.	Wales	Total
25,638	25,323.3	1,364.8	26,688.1	25,983.7	1.451	27,434.7
19,186	18,899.5	888.5	19,788	18,870.3	872	19,742.3
6,318	6,253.9	425.8	6,679.7	6,541.7	451	6,992.7
4,610.3	4,792.7	266.5	5,059.2	4,814.4	300	5,114.4
8,644.7	8,664	44.2	8,708.2	8,533.4	67	8,600.4
47,856.8	46,666.6	2,973	29,639.6	46,713.5	2,915	49,628.5
50,622.9	50,742	3,377.1	54,119.1	51,121.4	3,393	54,514.4
5,804.8	5,946.5	331.0	6,277.5	6,264.6	326	6,590.6
23,419.5	22,094.7	1,186.7	23,286.4	22,250.9	1,183	23,433.9
199,200.2	192,160	11,001.2	203,161	193,613.8	11,107	204,720.8

Percentage increase in staff 1971–77 = 75%. Percentage increase in staff 1972–77 = 39%

Total staff England 1972 = 134,524 (w.t.e.). Percentage increase in social work staff 1972–77 = 25%

(p. 60, *Health and Personal Social Services Statistics 1973*, HMSO 1973)

APPENDIX C
NUMBERS OF STUDENTS ENTERING TRAINING AND QUALIFYING

Student intakes 1972–80 (UK courses and Republic of Ireland)

	1972	1975	1977	1978	1979	1980
CQSW	2,855	3,582	4,039	3,787	3,736	3,790
CRSW	130	81	24	21	12	–
CSS	–	129	510	633	921	1,079
PQS	–	–	131	235	269	210

CCETSW Awards 1972–80

	1972	1975	1977	1978	1979	1980
CQSW	2,183	3,023	3,390	3,584	3,592	3,507
CRSW	73	104	52	21	22	12
CSS	–	–	71	150	205	483
Students completing PQS courses	–	–	36	118	116	150

Source: *CCETSW Data on Training for the Social Services 1979 and 1980*, CCETSW 1981.

Appendix D
GREAT BRITAIN POPULATION PROJECTIONS – MID-1979 BASE (THOUSANDS)

Age group	1979 (base)	1980	1981	1986	1991	1996	2001	2011	2019
0–14									
Males	5,974	5,861	5,763	5,521	5,865	6,339	6,377	5,828	6,056
Females	5,655	5,549	5,454	5,222	5,550	5,997	6,033	5,511	5,726
Persons	11,629	11,410	11,217	10,743	11,415	12,336	12,410	11,339	11,782
15–29									
Males	6,179	6,262	6,347	6,634	6,372	5,767	5,530	6,343	6,210
Females	5,910	5,976	6,046	6,325	6,075	5,493	5,261	6,033	5,907
Persons	12,089	12,238	12,393	12,959	12,447	11,260	101,791	12,376	12,117
30–44									
Males	5,231	5,293	5,335	5,567	5,830	6,050	6,331	5,477	5,384
Females	5,121	5,198	5,255	5,497	5,750	5,923	6,198	5,373	5,281
Persons	10,352	10,491	10,590	11,064	11,580	11,973	12,529	10,850	10,665
45–Ret*									
Males	5,983	5,935	5,918	5,813	5,810	6,149	6,374	7,157	7,279
Females	4,899	4,781	4,694	4,477	4,556	5,013	5,238	5,653	5,834
Persons	10,882	10,716	10,612	10,291	10,366	11,162	11,612	12,810	13,113
Over Ret†									
Males	3,141	3,176	3,184	3,222	3,290	3,258	3,187	3,278	3,639
Females	6,315	6,409	6,477	6,563	6,482	6,298	6,159	6,539	6,872
Persons	9,456	9,585	9,661	9,785	9,772	9,556	9,346	9,817	10,511
Persons all ages	54,408	54,440	54,473	54,842	55,580	56,287	56,688	57,192	58,188

* Males 64, Females 59   †Males 65, Females 60
Source: OPCS Monitor Office of Population Censuses and Surveys, 1980.

REFERENCES AND BIBLIOGRAPHY

Attlee, C., 1920, *The Social Worker*. Library of Social Service
Billis, D., Bromley, G., Hey, A. and Rowbottom, R., 1980, *Organising Social Services Departments*. Heinemann
Booth, T. A., 1979, *Planning for Welfare*. Blackwell and Robertson
Brearley, P., 1975, *Social Work Ageing and Society*. Routledge and Kegan Paul
Brearley, P., 1977, *Residential Work with the Elderly*. Routledge and Kegan Paul
Brewer, C. and Lait, J., 1980, *Can Social Work Survive*. Temple Smith
British Association of Social Workers, 1970, *Research Social Work*. BASW Monograph No. 4
British Association of Social Workers, 1976, *Social Work Education: The Way Ahead*.
British Association of Social Workers, 1977, *The Social Work Task*. BASW
British Association of Social Workers, 1979, *Social Work Education. The 1979 Position Statement*. BASW
British Association of Social Workers, 1980, *Clients are Fellow Citizens*. BASW
Brunel Institute of Organisation and Social Service, 1974, *Social Services Departments: Developing Patterns of Work and Organisation*. Heinemann
Butrym, Z. T., 1976, *The Nature of Social Work*. Macmillan
Central Council for Education and Training in Social Work, 1976, *Values in Social Work*. CCETSW 1973, *Residential Work is a Part of Social Work*. 1974, *Social Work. People with handicaps need better trained workers*. CCETSW 1975, *Day Services. An Action Plan for Training*. CCETSW 1975, *Education and Training for*

Social Work. CCETSW 1978, *Report Three. 1974-77.* CCETSW 1979, *Accreditation in Social Work.* CCETSW 1980, *The Certificate in Social Service: A Progress Report.* CCETSW 1980, *Data on Training for the Social Services.* CCETSW 1980, *Research and Practice.* CCETSW/PSSC

Central Health Services Council and Personal Social Services Council, 1978, *Collaboration in Community Care*: A Discussion Document. HMSO

Central Policy Review Staff, 1975, *A Joint Framework for Social Policies*, HMSO

Central Policy Review Staff, 1977, *Population and the Social Services.* HMSO

Central Statistical Office, 1979, *Social Trends, 9.* HMSO

Central Statistical Office, 1980, *Social Trends, 10.* HMSO

Clough, R., 1981, *Old Age Homes.* Allen and Unwin

Cmnd. 7746, 1979, *The Government Expenditure Plans, 1980-81.* HMSO

Cmnd. 7841, 1980, *The Government Expenditure Plans 1980-81 to 1983-84.* HMSO

Cypher, J. 1977, *Personal Social Services, Manpower and Training.* Social Workers Education Trust

Cypher, J. (ed.), 1979, *Seebohm Across Three Decades.* BASW Publications

Davies, M., 1981, *The Essential Social Worker.* Heinemann

Department of Applied Social Studies, University of Warwick, 1978, *Preparing for Social Work Practice.* University of Warwick

DES, 1973, *Social Work and the School.* HMSO

DHSS, 1975-80, *Supplementary Benefits Commission. Annual Reports 1975-80.* HMSO

DHSS, 1976, *Manpower and Training for the Social Services.* (Birch Report) HMSO

DHSS, 1976, *Priorities for Health and Personal Social Services in England.* HMSO

DHSS, 1977, *The Way Forward: Priorities in the Health and Personal Social Services.* HMSO

DHSS, 1978, *Social Service Teams: The Practitioners View.* HMSO

DHSS, 1979, *An Investigation into the Effect on Clients of Industrial Action by Social Workers in the London Borough of Tower Hamlets*

DHSS, 1980, *Health and Personal Social Service Statistics for England, 1978.* HMSO

DHSS, 1981, *Care in the Community: A Consultative Document on Moving Resources for Care in England.*

References and Bibliography

DHSS, 1981, *Care in Action: A Handbook of Policies and Priorities for the Health and Personal Social Services*. HMSO

England, H. (ed.), 1980, *Education for Co-operation in Health and Social Work*. Occasional Paper No. 4. Royal College of Practitioners

Financial Times, 1979, 'Planning in an age of uncertainty' *Financial Times*

George V. and Wilding, P., 1976, *Ideology and Social Welfare*. Routledge

Goldberg, E. M., 1970, *Helping the Aged*. Allen and Unwin

Goldberg, E. M. and Hatch, S., 1981, *A New Look at the Personal Social Services*. Policy Studies Institute, Discussion Paper No. 4

Goldberg, E. M. and Warburton, 1979, *Ends and Means in Social Work*. Allen and Unwin

Gough, I., 1979, *The Political Economy of the Welfare State*. Macmillan

Grimond, J., 1978, *The Common Welfare*. Temple Smith

Hadley, R. and McGrath, M. (eds), (1980), *Patch Based Social Service Teams*. Bulletin No. 2. University of Lancaster

Halmos, P., 1978, *The Personal and the Political*. Hutchinson

Harris, R. and Seldon, A., 1971, *Choice in Welfare*. Institute of Economic Affairs

Hey, A., 1979, 'Specialisation in Social Work' in J. Cypher (ed.), *Across Three Decades*. BSAW

Holme, A. and Maizel, J., 1978, *Social Workers and Volunteers*. BASW and Allen and Unwin

House of Commons Paper, 1978, *Eighth Report from the Expenditure Committee. Session 1977–78*. HMSO

House of Commons Paper, 1980, *Third Report from the Social Services Committee. Session 1979–80*. HMSO

Independent Commission on International Issues, 1980, *North-South. A Programme for Survival*. Pan Books

Jackson, M. P. and Valencia, B.M., 1979, *Financial Aid Through Social Work*. Routledge

Judge, K., 1978, *Rationing in the Social Services*. Heinemann

Judge, K. (ed.), 1980, *Pricing the Social Services*. Macmillan

Keith-Lucas, A., 1957, *Decisions about People in Need*. Chapel Hill

Kendall, K. A. (ed.), 1970, *Social Work Values in an Age of Discontent*. Council on Social Work Education. (USA)

Marshall, M., Preston-Sheet, M. and Wincott, E. (eds), 1979, *Teamwork, For and Against*. BASW Publications

McDermott, F. E. (ed.), 1978, *Self-determination in Social Work*. Routledge and Kegan Paul
Meadows, D et al. 1972, *Limits to Growth*. Universe Books
Midgley, 1981 *Professional Imperialism. Social Work in the Third World*. Heinemann
Ministry of Health, 1959, Report of the Working Party on Social Workers in the Local Authority Health and Welfare Services. (Younghusband Report). HMSO
Mishra, R., 1977, *Society and Social Policy*. Macmillan
OECD, 1979, *Interfutures: Facing the Future*. OECD, Paris
OECD, 1981, *The Welfare State in Crisis*. OECD, Paris
Olsen, R. (ed.), 1974, *Management in the Social Services: The Team Leader's Task*. University of North Wales. Bangor
Olsen, M. R. (ed.), 1978 *The Unitary Model*. BASW Publications
P. A. Management Consultants Ltd., 1972, *An Evaluation of Future Social Services Expenditure on Behalf of the City of Leicester*
Parry, N., Rustin, M. and Satyamurti (eds), 1979, *Social Work, Welfare and the State*. Edward Arnold
Parsloe, P., 1978, *Social Service Teams. The Practitioners View*. HMSO
Parsloe, P., 1981, *Social Service Teams*. Allen and Unwin
Payne, M., 1979, *Power, Authority and Responsibility in Social Services: Social Work in Area Teams*. Macmillan
Personal Social Services Council, 1976, *Voluntary Social Service Manpower Resources*. PSSC
Personal Social Services Council, 1976, *Complaints, Procedures; the Personal Social Services*. PSSC
Personal Social Services Council and The Health Education Council, 1976, *Relationships Between Health and Social Education*. PSSC
Personal Social Services Council, 1977, *Residential Care Reviewed*. PSSC
Personal Social Services Council, 1977, *Personal Social Services: Basic Information*. PSSC
Personal Social Services Council, 1979, *A Future for Intermediate Treatment*. PSSC
Personal Social Services Council, 1980 *Setting a Target Date*. PSSC
Personal Social Services Council, 1980, *Cuts in Local Authority Spending on Personal Social Services*. PSSC
Pinker, R., 1979, *The Idea of Welfare*. Heinemann
Rees, S., 1978, *Social Work Face to Face*. Edward Arnold
Report of the Committee on Local Authority and Allied Personal

References and Bibliography

Social Services (Seebohm Report), 1968, *Cmnd. 3703*. HMSO
Residential Care Association, 1979, *The Social Work Task*. RCA
Residential Care Association, 1980, *A New Approach to Training*. RCA
Rostow, W. W., 1979, *Getting from Here to There*. Macmillan
Rowlings, C., 1981, *Social Work with Elderly People*. Allen and Unwin
Seed, P., 1973, *The Expansion of Social Work*. Routledge
Seldon, A., 1977, *Charge*, Temple Smith
Simpson, T., 1978, *Advocacy and Social Change*. National Institute for Social Work
Social Work Service, 1979, *An Investigation into the Effects on Clients of Industrial Action by Social Workers in the London Borough of Tower Hamlets*. DHSS
Specht, H., 1976, *Community Development Projects*. NISW
Specht, H., and Vickery, H., 1977, *Integrating Social Work Methods*. Allen and Unwin
Stevenson, O., 1973, *Claimant or Client?* Allen and Unwin
Stevenson, O., 1981, *Specialisation in Social Service Teams*. Allen and Unwin
Strentfield, D., and Wilson, T., 1980, *Information on Social Services Departments*. Joint Unit for Social Services Research, University of Sheffield
Titmuss, R. M., 1950, *Problems of Social Policy*. HMSO
Townsend, P., 1979 *Poverty*. Penguin
Unell, J., 1979, *Voluntary Social Services: Financial Resources*. Bedford Square Press
Walton, R., 1975, 'Welfare Rights and Social Work', Chapter 7, in H. Jones (ed.), *Towards a New Social Work*. Routledge
Walton, R., 1975, *Women in Social Work*. Routledge
Walton, R. and Elliott, D. (eds), 1980, *Residential Care: A Reader in Current Theory and Practice*. Pergamon
Weir, S., 1981, 'What do people think about Social Workers?' *New Society*, 7 May
Welsh Office, 1979, *Health and Personal Social Service Statistics for Wales, No. 6*. HMSO
Williams, G. (Chairman) 1967, *Caring for People*. Allen and Unwin
Wolfenden Report, 1977, *Report of the Committee on the Future of Voluntary Organisations*. Croom Helm
Wootton, B., 1959, *Social Science and Social Pathology*. Allen and Unwin
Younghusband, E., 1947, *Report on the Employment and Training of*

Social Workers. T. A. Constable
Younghusband, E., 1951, *Social Work in Britain.* T. A. Constable
Younghusband, E., 1978, *Social Work in Britain 1950–75* Two volumes. Allen and Unwin

INDEX

accountability, 75, 89–90
administration, 35, 40, 52, 55, 56, 82, 92–3
advice, 34, 39, 51, 70
advocacy, 35, 40, 54, 56, 57, 85, 87
Age Concern, 25
assessment, 34, 48–50, 58, 59
Attlee, C., 34, 37

Birch Report, 50, 55, 59, 62, 77
Brandt Report, 4
Brearley, P., 61
Brewer, C., 47
British Association of Social Workers, 24, 35, 37, 50, 55, 75, 90
bureaucracy, 47, 48, 69

casework, 50, 54, 81, 93
Central Council for Education and Training in Social Work, 37, 62, 63, 76, 81
Certificate of Qualification in Social Work, 66, 76–9 *passim*, 81, 82
Certificate of Social Service, 77, 78, 80, 82
charging, 27
Cheshire Homes, 25
Children and Young Persons Acts, 1963 and 1969, 45
Chronically Sick and Disabled Persons Act, 1970, 62, 74
Citizens' Advice Bureau, 25, 26
Clough, R., 61
community care, 21, 29, 43
community work, 54, 57, 70
confidentiality, 88

coordination, 7, 21, 26, 29, 37–8, 43, 69, 88
counselling, 51–2, 53, 57
C.P.A.G., 25

Davies, M., 50
Department of Health and Social Security, 22, 28, 43, 48
Dr Barnado's, 25

economic development, 5, 6, 7, 9–15, 85–7
education, 12, 13, 20, 35, 40, 41, 42, 46, 85
energy, 5

Family Service Units, 25

Goldberg, M., 35, 75
Gough, I., 15
Grimond, J., 33

Halmos, P., 85
Harris, R., 28
health, 12, 13, 20, 21, 28, 40–3 *passim*, 46, 61, 85–7 *passim*
Hey, A., 74
Holme, A., 24
housing, 7, 12, 13, 18, 20, 21, 28, 35, 40, 41, 42, 85, 87, 88

information, 34, 37, 39, 51, 70
Institute of Economic Affairs, 27, 92
intake teams, 38
integrated methods, 50–1

Index

Judge, K., 28

Keith-Lucas, A., 92
Kondratieff, 5

Lait, J., 47
Local Authority Social Services Act, 1970, 45

Maizel, J., 24
Maria Colwell, 67
Marxism, vii, 7, 37, 47, 90, 91
Mental Health Act, 1959, 45, 62
MIND, 25

National Children's Home, 25
National Institute of Social Work, vi, 35
National Society for the Prevention of Cruelty to Children, 25

Organisation for Economic Cooperation and Development, 2–5 *passim*, 9, 11, 84, 87
outposting, 38, 39, 43

Parsloe, P., 73
participation, 5, 6, 59, 76, 89, 91, 92
patch system, 70
Payne, M., 73
personal social services, 2, 6, 11, 12, 13, 16–32, 33, 47, 62, 80, 85–7 *passim*, 89, 92
Personal Social Services Council, 30
planning, 2, 29
political institutions, 5, 8, 56, 70
population, 2, 3, 5, 16–19
Post-Qualifying Studies, 76, 77, 79, 82
prevention, 45
priorities, 14,
private welfare, 6, 14, 15, 26–7, 29, 85, 87
public expenditure, 11–13

research, 14, 67, 68, 89
residential care, 21, 22, 27, 31, 35, 57–60, 63, 68, 71, 76, 77
Richmond Fellowship, 25
Rostow, W., 5, 92
Rowlings, C., 61

Seebohm Report, 20

Seldon, A., 28
self-determination, 88, 91
service groups
  children and young people, 6, 17–18, 20, 21, 27, 31, 35, 40, 60, 63
  elderly, 12, 18–20 *passim*, 22, 27, 31, 35, 42, 57, 60
  ethnic minorities, 12, 18
  mentally ill, 12, 18, 20, 22, 27, 35, 40, 57, 60, 63
  mentally handicapped, 6, 12, 18, 20–2 *passim*, 27, 35, 42, 57, 60
  physically handicapped, 6, 12, 18, 20, 27, 35, 42, 57, 60
  single-parent families, 12, 19
social change, 18, 55, 91
social development, 7
social group work, 53–4, 57, 93
social policy, 20–1
social problems, 19–20, 56
social security, 7, 12, 13, 18, 28, 35, 41, 42, 43, 85, 86, 87
social services cuts, 19, 26, 30–1
social services departments, 33, 35, 51, 52, 63, 68, 69
social welfare, 2
social work, 33–44
  functions, 33–7, 45, 55–7, 58, 84
  manpower, 62–7
  relationships to other services, 37–44
  scenarios, 84–8
  training, 60, 63, 74–8
Social Work (Scotland) Act, 1968, 45
Specht, H., 21, 50
specialisation, 38, 50, 51, 69, 73–4, 80
Stevenson, O., 73
supplementary benefit, 20, 21

teams, 71–3
technology, 4
Third World, 4, 8
Titmuss, R., 34
Townsend, P., 19

unemployment, 6, 8, 10, 12, 14, 18, 85, 86

values, 2, 5, 9, 37, 88–93
Vickery, A., 50

107

voluntary organisations, 15, 25–6, 88
volunteers, 22–5, 55, 88
voucher schemes, vii, 92

Weir, S., 47
welfare rights, 40

Welfare State, 5–7 *passim*, 9–15, 16, 21, 33, 85, 86, 87
Wolfenden Report, 24, 26
Wootton, B., 92

Younghusband, E., 62